NATIONAL POLICE LIBRARY

20030840

NATIONAL POLICE LIBRARY

D1149921

HOW TO PASS

THE CIVIL SERVICE QUALIFYING TESTS

2ND EDITION

NATIONAL
POLICE
LIBRARY

DISCARDED

NATIONAL LIBRARY

Mike Bryon

**KOGAN
PAGE**

Acc. no. 20030840

Classmark _ _ _ 351.3 _ _ _ _ _ _

BRY
_ _ _ _ _ _ _ _

First published in 1995
Reprinted 1997, 1998, 1999
Second edition 2003

Apart from any fair dealing for the purposes of research or private study, or criticism or review, as permitted under the Copyright, Designs and Patents Act 1988, this publication may only be reproduced, stored or transmitted, in any form or by any means, with the prior permission in writing of the publishers, or in the case of reprographic reproduction in accordance with the terms and licences issued by the CLA. Enquiries concerning reproduction outside these terms should be sent to the publishers at the undermentioned address:

Kogan Page Limited
120 Pentonville Road
London N1 9JN
United Kingdom
www.kogan-page.co.uk

© Mike Bryon, 1995, 2003

The right of Mike Bryon to be identified as the author of this work has been asserted by him in accordance with the Copyright, Designs and Patents Act 1988.

British Library Cataloguing in Publication Data

A CIP record for this book is available from the British Library.

ISBN 0 7494 3793 6

Typeset by Saxon Graphics Ltd, Derby
Printed and bound in Great Britain by Clays Ltd, St Ives plc

Contents

Acknowledgements

I owe thanks to Joan Ballington, Ed Hateley, Jasna Medvedovic-Duricic and Kate Stephenson for contributing many practice questions. Their contribution makes the title a far better source of practice and a much better book. The views expressed and any errors are entirely my own.

Preface

This text aims to provide advice and practice relevant to the tests used to recruit administrators to many departments and agencies in the United Kingdom Civil Service. The practice exercises are intended to help build up speed and accuracy and confidence in these widely used qualifying exams. The material is intended to help the reader reach the standard demanded by these tests. It does not, therefore, always reflect the difficulty of the questions or the same competencies examined in the real tests.

It is common for job seekers to take measures to improve their CV or interview technique, but relatively few seek to improve their performance in employers' tests. Too few candidates realize that they can improve their scores. Occupational psychologists accept that a lack of familiarity with tests, low self-esteem, nervousness or a lack of confidence will result in a lower score. It is equally true to say that hard work, determination and, most of all, systematic preparation can lead to an improvement in performance.

This book has been developed expressly for the purpose of helping candidates prepare for the Civil Service Qualifying Exams. Clearly if you face one of these tests then this specialist title promises to be of great help. However, before you use this book you must establish that the types of question are indeed relevant to the test that you face. The department or agency to whom you have applied should have sent you a description of the test. Alternatively, it may have a Web site that provides information. It is essential that you study this document or information carefully and, before you spend time on these exercises, establish that this book contains material relevant to the real questions.

It is recommended that you do not rely solely on this title as a source of practice material. There are many other good volumes on the market, and this book should only be one of a number that you utilize in your preparation for a Civil Service qualifying test.

If you are finding it difficult to identify relevant material then by all means write to me care of Kogan Page, enclosing details of the test that you face and a telephone number or e-mail address on which you can be contacted, and I will be glad to inform you of any other source that I know.

I apologize in advance if you discover any errors in these practice questions; try not to allow it to undermine your confidence in the value of practice. I have tried hard to keep errors out and I hope I have not missed too many. I will be glad to hear of any, care of Kogan Page, in order that they can be removed at the next reprint.

The Civil Service, the Tests and Practice

Administrative staff in the Civil Service

Civil Servants are officials who work for a Minister of the government of the day. They work in departments and agencies of central government, developing and implementing policies. Employees of the police, local government and the armed services are not Civil Servants.

Civil Servants are politically impartial and the Service is non-political. Governments change but the service remains unaffected and will serve whichever government is elected.

Administrators in the Service are in an important respect considered to be generalist. After a qualifying period, and once you reach the higher grades, you may gain experience of all aspects of administration and move between specialist functions periodically. The experience gained from each function is considered to be transferable, and you will be expected to be able to learn quickly and to be flexible. Training is primarily on the job. The key functions include work in, for example, a registry, a secretariat, a finance section, a personnel or training department or a computing unit.

In recent years the Service has undergone considerable change, and previously centrally defined structures no longer necessarily apply throughout the Service. Increasingly, Civil Servants are occupied with the development and implementation of the policies of the European Union as well as those of Parliament.

A major effort has been made to locate parts of departments and most of the executive agencies outside the capital. This has meant that fewer Civil Servants are located in London and the South East region generally.

Another change has been the provision of information about the Service and vacancies on the World Wide Web. This is a vital source of considerable information for any prospective candidate, especially in terms of information about the type of work available and the recruitment process, including any test. The Web makes it far easier to keep the information up to date and provides a very cost-effective means of providing a great deal of information. There is little point in attempting to repeat or summarize this material here. See 'Further information' for useful Web addresses.

Up until now, the terms and conditions of employment of Civil Servants have been explained in a substantial, rigorous and clearly written publication called *The Civil Service Staff Handbook*. Although in recent years the prospects of promotion have reduced considerably, all staff benefit from annual appraisals which include an assessment of whether or not the individual is fit for promotion.

It is a legal requirement that recruitment to the Service is by fair and open competition and that selection and promotion are on the basis of merit alone. Fairness and openness mean that the Service is required to ensure that vacancies are widely publicized, and consequently, this often results in very large numbers of applications. To ensure fairness each applicant must be given proper and due consideration, which takes a considerable amount of time and resources. In general, the recruitment process in the Service comprises the following features:

- All applicants are sent, or referred to Web sites that provide, information about the vacancies and department. The intention is that this allows candidates to make an informed decision over whether or not to proceed with their application.
- Application forms are used (some are online) that obtain sufficient information to afford a sift against a set of criteria agreed in advance and considered essential to the post. It is common for many candidates to be rejected at the application form stage, so take care to present your experience as relevant and minimize the number of errors on your form.
- Candidates who pass the application form sift may be required to pass a set of standardized tests which are administered to large groups of applicants at a time. Some tests are computerized, some are paper and pencil. In many cases as many as 80 per cent of candidates are rejected at the testing stage.
- Candidates who have successfully passed these sifts may be required to attend a two-day event at an assessment centre where they undertake work-related exercises.
- Panel interviews are conducted.

The Service is an acknowledged leader in the field of providing childcare support, career break schemes and job-sharing arrangements. I have first-hand experience of working with Civil Servants who take equality of opportunity very seriously and work hard to ensure a fair and equitable system of recruitment and management.

There have been considerable and genuine efforts, coordinated by the Cabinet Office, to address issues of representation. However, despite these best efforts, black and other minority people within the Service are still more likely to be employed in clerical grades. Also the proportion of women in higher managerial posts is lower than the total should be if the sexes were proportionally represented.

The Cabinet Office continually monitors the Service's recruitment processes, including the qualifying exams, for bias, and takes measures to guard against any unintentional racial or gender discrimination. No system is perfect, but candidates should take some assurance from the fact that the Service is ahead of the majority of British industries, operates a relatively equitable recruitment process, and represents a better employer than most.

A programme of validity studies are carried out to demonstrate that the selected candidates go on to be successful in the Civil Service.

On the issue of equality of opportunity and the Fast Stream Qualifying Test, a review report of the Fast Stream dated September 2001 reported that:

- Women formed nearly half the total number of applicants and in 2000 formed a greater proportion of successful candidates.
- Candidates who described their ethnicity as black or as belonging to an ethnic minority group were disproportionately unsuccessful at the Qualifying Test stage.
- People with a disability were successful in broadly the same proportions as they applied, but only a small number applied in the first instance.

The *Fast Stream Recruitment Report 2001–2002* recognized that there was still much to do, but found some progress over the previous year in the realizing of equality in representation of individuals drawn from ethnic minority groups. The report found that the number of ethnic minority candidates appointed to the programme had increased to 7.6 per cent of the total appointed from a previous year figure of 6.8 per cent.

Tests and practice

When tests are used to select and reject applicants, they leave the candidate with no alternative but to try to earn the very best possible score. Two things will help you to do this. First, realize that practice prior to the test will help you to become familiar with the test demands, build up speed and avoid common mistakes. Second, you must realize that doing well in a test is not simply down to intelligence but also requires you to be sufficiently motivated to want to pass and to try hard. In some cases, practice and a determination to do well will mean the difference between pass and fail.

All employers' tests, including those used by the Civil Service, owe much of their heritage to attempts early in the last century to measure intelligence. We are all familiar with the notion of IQ (intelligence quotient) and how a score is offered as a measurement of an individual's intelligence; a score of 100 is deemed average, while a score of over 160 might indicate genius. Pioneers of testing predicted that we would no longer have to wait for the effects of experience to discover how well suited an individual was for a particular career or educational path. Instead we would be able to attribute to an individual a score and be able to tell who was best suited for a particular career or for a place in, for example, higher education.

It was soon realized that these early tests failed to predict success in particular careers or higher education. Intelligence is a complex and controversial notion which has proved very difficult to define. The concept of intelligence adopted by the early testers was crude, and only a few items that are propertied to make up this complex term were employed. The early tests were primarily concerned with the measurement of verbal ability and the handling of numerical, pictorial and geometric relations.

The overstatement of the validity of these early tests gave rise to considerable scepticism and some hostility towards testing. There had, of course, been more sober commentators, and the views of these individuals came to the fore. In particular, it was stressed that an individual's score should be taken not as an indication of overall intelligence, but instead simply as a measurement of that individual's ability in the aptitude tested. Some IQ tests were renamed ability tests and redesigned to measure more specifically single aptitudes. Instead of attributing a single score, a profile of scores in each ability was offered. In other cases an individual's score was compared with the normal score of other candidates with similar backgrounds. These tests are in essence the precursors of the tests used today by employers. Considerable and lengthy studies are undertaken in order to quantify the predictive value of such tests.

Recruitment is a notoriously subjective business. Handwriting analysis, personality questionnaires, application forms, references and interviews all fail to discriminate objectively between candidates. The best we can say is that some of these methods are less subjective than others.

The occupational psychologist, however, goes to considerable lengths to achieve objectivity, and he or she does this by applying standard scientific methods and statistical techniques to the task of deciding between candidates. The resulting psychometric tests are considered by many to be the best single predictor of likely job performance. This is not to say that tests are perfect. In fact, the vast majority are imperfect because for most positions, job performance is ill defined. Things are made worse because the content of most tests – the questions – does not exactly measure the behavioural traits under investigation. It also inadvertently measures traits that are irrelevant to the post.

As a test candidate, the most important thing you should realize about these imperfections is that they will produce what are called 'false negatives' and 'false positives'. This means that an imperfect test will underestimate the potential of some candidates and overestimate the potential of others. Someone capable of doing the job, who is falsely attributed a low score, and whose application is then rejected, is called a false negative. If candidates achieve scores greater than their true potential, and as a result are passed through to the next stage of the process, they are called false positives.

Notification that you were unsuccessful may therefore mean nothing more than that you were a false negative. You should certainly not conclude that failure to pass a qualifying exam means that you are unsuitable for employment as a Civil Servant. In some instances so many people apply for a position and there are so few vacancies that even the very able are rejected. So do not immediately rethink your career plans if you fail a qualifying exam. Try again after undertaking more practice. If you repeatedly fail, try to establish if any alternative routes exist into the employment of your choice. It may be that holders of particular qualifications do not have to sit the exam, or you may be able to join the department at a more junior grade and seek promotion.

The best frame of mind in which to approach a qualifying exam is to treat it as an opportunity to demonstrate your true worth. Avoid any feelings of resentment over the fact that you have to take a test. Do not fear failure but instead concentrate on the opportunity to pass. Have confidence in yourself. Realize that you have nothing to lose if you try your best and really go for it.

Practice before a qualifying exam is essential, and can make a significant difference to your score. It is obvious that practice will help. It will mean that you make fewer mistakes and work more quickly against the often tight time constraints. It will ensure you are familiar with the test demands, and that you revise forgotten rules and develop a good test technique.

If passing is important to you, you should be prepared to make a major commitment in terms of setting time aside to practise during the weeks leading up to the test. You can be sure that other candidates will make such a commitment, so if you do not, you risk coming a poor second. To maximize the benefits of practice you should undertake two types:

1.   You should practise in a relaxed situation, without time constraints, on questions which are similar to those described in the department's test description booklet or Web page. The aim is to realize the test demands and work out why you got a question wrong. This way you revise the competencies and build up confidence in your own abilities.

2.   Then practise on realistic questions against a strict time limit and in circumstances as realistic to the test as you can manage. The aim is to get used to answering the questions under the pressure of time and to build up speed and accuracy.

You should aim to undertake a minimum of 12 hours' practice, and as much as 20 hours if you can obtain sufficient practice material. Restrict your practice to questions similar to the real thing.

2

Practice for Clerical Tests

Considerable decentralization has taken place in the type of qualifying exam used to recruit to clerical positions in the Civil Service. In the 1990s nationwide tests were applied to almost every department or agency of government for the recruitment of clerical and executive positions. Today only the Fast Stream remains as a national test, while for lower grades, departments and agencies have done their own thing. Most continue to use tests as a part of the recruitment process to these positions, and there remains considerable similarity between the competencies examined and the types of question used.

The following practice questions are typical of the type used to recruit to clerical positions. However, check their relevance to the particular test that you face before you spend time working through the material.

If you have never sat a psychometric test before, then in order to get some idea of what to expect you must think back to the days of examinations at school or university. You will attend a test centre with a room either set out as an examination hall with small desks, or with banks of computer terminals, depending on whether you face a paper and pen or computer-administered version of the test.

Other candidates are very likely to be present. In some instances there may be a lot of other candidates. A test administrator will welcome you and explain the process. He or she will be following a prepared script, and will be happy to answer any questions, although the answers given may be rather brief or superficial. This is because the administrator is keen that all candidates (including those who have attended on other days and will not have heard your question) receive the same information and experience the same test conditions, so he or she will be reluctant to stray far from the script.

If you suffer a disability that may affect your performance in the test, or that means you require things to be organized in a different way, contact the organization that has invited you straight away.

The types of practice question in this chapter

The questions in any real test are almost certain to be multiple choice or short answer, and the test will be a type of competition where you must compete for one of the places against other candidates. This chapter offers practice in the types of question listed below. The next chapter provides further practice for each type under mock test conditions:

- Handling data: the essentials (38 questions).
- Quantitative reasoning (29 questions).
- Data interpretation (34 questions).
- Word swap (19 questions).
- Missing words (21 questions).
- Correct sentences (20 questions).

Sources of other practice material are listed in 'Further information'.

Handling data: the essentials

You should be able to answer these questions without a calculator in under 10 seconds. Once you manage that, you should practise some more until you can answer them in five seconds! So get practising. There is no better way to improve your speed and accuracy in this key competency.

Try the following 38 questions.

1. Orlando is facing south. If he turns through one right angle anticlockwise, in which direction will he face?

    Answer:

2. Allegra is facing north and turns through three right angles in a clockwise direction. In what direction does she now face?

    Answer:

3. Greg turns through two right angles in a clockwise direction. He ends up facing south. In which direction was he originally facing?

    Answer:

4. David is lost. He set off this morning walking due west and from the sun's position can tell that he is now facing due east. He knows he made two right-angled turns. Can you tell if he turned clockwise or anticlockwise from the information given?

    Answer:

5.   A store sells batteries for £3.00 for a pack of four. What is the cost of each battery?

Answer: [   ]

6.   A store sells batteries for £3.00 for a pack of four. How many batteries will you get for £21?

Answer: [   ]

7.   A shop sells batteries for £1.33 each. How much will four cost?

Answer: [   ]

8.   A shop sells batteries for £1.50. What is the cost of 12?

Answer: [   ]

9.   A supermarket needs 48 till rolls for a usual Saturday's trading. The rolls come in packs of three. How many packs will the store use?

Answer: [   ]

10. Eggs are sold in boxes of six for £1.56. How much will 24 eggs cost?

Answer: [   ]

11. Eggs are sold in boxes of six for £1.56. How much will 20 eggs cost? (Assume that the store will split a box.)

Answer: [   ]

12. A medium-sized egg weighs 60 gm. How much do the eggs weigh in a box of six?

Answer: [   ]

13. The small-sized eggs in a box of six weigh in total 300 gm. How much would four eggs from the box weigh?

Answer: [   ]

14. Lola raised £132 for charity by giving sponsored Italian language lessons. She charges £12 a lesson, so how many lessons did she give?

Answer: [   ]

15. Hope was sponsored 30p for each length that she swam. She raised a total of £12.00. How many lengths did she manage to swim?

Answer: [   ]

16. A kilo of parmesan cheese costs £16.00. How much would a piece that weighed 550 gm cost?

Answer: [   ]

17. 400 gm of beans comprises 1600 beans. How much does each bean weigh?

Answer: [   ]

18. Ten piles each comprise 37 individual beans with an average weight of 0.3 gm. How much do the 10 piles of beans weigh in total?

Answer: [   ]

19. Douglas purchased 25 kilos of potatoes at 28p a kilo. How much did he spend?

Answer: [   ]

20. An electricity bill is calculated by a charge of 10.1p for each unit of power used. How much would the charge be if you had used 660 units?

Answer: [   ]

21. VAT on electricity charges of £ 48.00 is calculated at 5 per cent. How much VAT will be added to the charge?

Answer: [   ]

22. 20 per cent of men responded positively when asked whether or not they hated Mondays. If the total survey comprised 60 men, how many responded positively to the question?

Answer: [   ]

23. A bus is timetabled to arrive at a terminus every three minutes. How many should arrive during a four-hour shift?

Answer: [   ]

24. Ella counted 30 aeroplanes going over her house in a six-hour period. How many minutes separated each plane? (Assume the intervals were equal.)

Answer: [   ]

25. 13 staff out of a workforce of 39 were late to work on the day of the train drivers' strike. What percentage of the workers were late that day?

Answer: [   ]

26. If this exercise were to comprise a total of 45 questions and you were allowed 10 seconds to attempt each, how long would the exercise last?

Answer: [   ]

27. Nine people ate at a restaurant and agreed to share the bill equally. The bill totalled £202.50. How much did each have to contribute?

Answer: [   ]

28. You agreed to pay half the cost of a carpet for a room with an area of 4 square metres at a cost of £30 per metre. What is the value of your contribution?

Answer: [   ]

29. You have agreed to a 12 per cent service charge on a bill of £112. How much extra will the cost be?

Answer: [   ]

30. VAT is levelled at 17.5 per cent on the net cost of sales totalling £12,000. Is it correct that the cost of the VAT will be over £2,000?

Answer: [   ]

31. What is 324 divided by 12?

Answer: [   ]

32. If VAT is levied at 17.5 per cent, is it correct that £262,500 of tax would be payable on sales of one and a half million?

Answer: [   ]

33. The instructions on a bottle recommend that you mix the contents with water at a ratio of 1:5. How much water should you add to 225 ml of the bottle's contents?

Answer: [   ]

34. If a train left at 11.35 am on a journey that normally takes 3 hours 20 minutes, but arrived 30 minutes late, what was its eventual time of arrival?

Answer: [   ]

35. If the Sterling/euro exchange rate is 1:1.53, how many euros would you receive in exchange for £20?

Answer: [   ]

36. If an apartment in Venice was sold for 500,000 euros would the vendor receive more or less than £320,000 if the Sterling/euro exchange rate was 1:1.53?

Answer: [   ]

37. By how many would the pig population grow if a sow was to have a litter of nine, and each of her offspring was to grow up and also have a first litter of nine?

Answer: [   ]

38. In 2002 there were 530 secondary schools in Greater London. The government wanted to increase this total by 16 schools. What approximate percentage increase does this represent?

Answer: [   ]

Quantitative reasoning

Attempt these questions without a calculator. Practise until you are able to answer each in under 30 seconds. Thirty examples are given.

1. If a dozen pens cost £1.20, how much are three and a half dozen?

   A £3.20   B £32   C £4.20   D £2.20   E £2.40   F£3.10

   Answer: [   ]

2. Two identical parcels weigh 0.5 kg. A parcel and a letter weigh 0.35 kg. How much do two letters weigh?

   A 0.25 kg   B 0.1 kg   C 0.15 kg   D 0.2 kg   E 0.3 kg
   F 0.5 kg

   Answer: [   ]

3. A company took advantage of a special offer and bought an overhead projector for one-third of its full price. How much was the discount?

   A 25%   B 66.66%   C 60%   D 33.33%   E 30%
   F 20%

   Answer: [   ]

4.   In the year 2000, a company made a profit totalling £24,840. In 2001 the profit increased by one quarter. How much profit did the company make in 2001?

A £6,210   B £30,050   C £5,210   D £32,050   E £32,240
F £31,050

Answer: [   ]

5.   In March Rob made 64 calls from his mobile, and his bill for March was £16. In April Rob made 25 per cent fewer calls. How many calls did Rob make in April, and how much was his bill?

A 16 / £4   B 48 / £12   C 38/ £12   D 32 / £12   E 32 / £6
F 34 / £4

Answer: [   ]

6.   The total business revenue for the year 2000 was £277,000. Staff wages were £67,000, overheads were £21,000 and production cost was £103,000. How much profit did the company make in the year 2000?

A £262,000   B £87,000   C £98,000   D £86,000
E £96,000   F £106,000

Answer: [   ]

7.   Mary is organizing transport for 150 conference attendees. If three coaches can accommodate 75 passengers, how many coaches should Mary hire?

A 3   B 2   C 4   D 6   E 5   F 7

Answer: [   ]

8. The total amount of money generated by ticket sales for a conference is £ 1,134.00. The conference hall can accommodate 126 people. Assuming they all bought a ticket and paid the same price, how much was the price of a single ticket?

A £9 B £11 C £8.50 D £10.50 E £7 F £8.50

Answer: [   ]

9. Sophie works Monday to Friday. She leaves her house at 6.15 am to arrive to work at 7.45. It takes her just as long to get back home in the evening. How much time does she spend commuting per week?

A 13 h B 14.15 h C 7.30 h D 15 h E 5 h F 15.30 h

Answer: [   ]

10. Last week Ann worked 2 h overtime, Fred worked 1.30 h overtime, Lisa worked 1 h overtime, Mary worked 2.30 h overtime and Bob worked 3 h overtime. How many hours overtime did they work on average?

A 10 h B 3 h C 2.32 h D 2.30 h E 2 h F 3.32 h

Answer: [   ]

11. Phil is earning £70 and his wife Rose £80 per week. Phil receives a 5 per cent pay rise and Rose decides to work only part time, so she is earning 45 per cent less than before. How much is their new combined income per week?

A £109.50 B £108.10 C £116.10 D £117.50
E £110.00 F £197.50

Answer: [   ]

12. A petty cash box contains 7 x 50p coins, 18 x 20p coins, 33 x 10p coins, 12 x 5p coins and 15 x 2p coins. How much money in total is in the petty cash box?

A £23.10   B £20.10   C £21.10   D £12.30   E £15.30
F £11.30

Answer: [   ]

13. 24 per cent of the staff working for a company are self-employed; the remainder are employed by the company directly. Of those directly employed, 18 per cent of the total staff work full time, while 29 members of staff are employed on a part-time basis. How many members of staff are self-employed?

A 36   B 29   C 48   D 18   E 9   F 12

Answer: [   ]

14. The total capital invested into a partnership is £70,000. Partner A invested 2.5 times more than partner B. How much money did partner B invest?

A £25,000   B £50,000   C £28,000   D £20,000
E £9,800   F £19,800

Answer: [   ]

15. If one photocopier can produce 180 copies per hour, how many copies can two photocopiers produce in 25 minutes?

A 125   B 175   C 150   D 145   E 75   F 200

Answer: [   ]

16. Angela spends 7 h per day in the office. She spends 3/7 of her time typing letters. How much time does Angela spend typing letters per week?

A 15 h   B 7.30 h   C 20 h   D 20.30 h   E 15.30 h   F 12 h

Answer: _____

17. A carpet cleaning company charges £2.25 per sq m. How much would it cost to clean a wall-to-wall carpet in an office sized 12 m by 18.5 m?

A £222   B £202   C £499.50   D £555   E £495
F £495.50

Answer: _____

18. Hasan earns £400 per week before tax. His tax is £64 per week. In percentage terms, how much tax is Hasan paying?

A 25%   B 64%   C 17.5%   D 8%   E 12%   F 16%

Answer: _____

19. An architect constructed a model of a shopping centre using a scale 1:2000. If the model is 57.5 cm long, how long will the actual shopping centre be when built?

A 11, 500 m   B 1,250 m   C 115 m   D 1,150 m
E 115,000.00 m   F 125 m

Answer: _____

20. In an office, the ratio of male to female workers is 1:3.5. If there are four male workers, how many females work in the office?

A 10   B 12   C 14   D 8   E 18   F 13

Answer: _____

21. Mojisola is taking a business trip to Italy. If the exchange rate for pounds Sterling to euros is 1:1.6, and she needs €400 per day, how many pounds should Mojisola exchange for a four-day stay?

    A £857 B £750 C £849.50 D £1000 E £600 F £500

    Answer: [   ]

22. John earns £18,700 pa. Sarah earns £28,000 pa. How much is Mark earning pa if he earns 47 per cent less than John and Sarah together?

    A £24,751 B £20,959 C £18,959 D £21,959
    E £21,949 F £22,949

    Answer: [   ]

23. The profit for the year 1999 was £1,250. If the profit increases by 10 per cent each year, how much profit will be made in the year 2001?

    A £1,500 B £1,512.5 C £1,650 D £1,525 E £15,125
    F £1,652

    Answer: [   ]

24. The population in an area is represented by a ratio of 3:7 young to old inhabitants. If a company wishes to reflect the same ratio among its employees and the company requires 370 employees, how many of them should be old?

    A 259 B 111 C 255 D 198 E 220 F 225

    Answer: [   ]

25. To reach its annual target, a sales team has to achieve on average 150 sales per quarter. At the end of the third quarter the sales are averaging 137 per quarter. How many

sales must the sales team achieve during the final quarter to reach the target?

A 211   B 123   C 189   D 150   E 137   F 411

Answer: [   ]

26. A secretary earns £15,400 pa after paying 23 per cent tax. How much is her annual income before tax?

A £20,000   B £17,220   C £24,780   D £15,376
E £16,450   F £18,881

Answer: [   ]

27. Company A employs twice as many people as Company B. Company C employs 25 per cent fewer people than Company A. If Company C employs 120, how many people does Company B employ?

A 75   B 60   C 150   D 120   E 80   F 160

Answer: [   ]

28. The size of an office is 11 m by 12.5 m. How many carpet tiles sized 50 cm by 50 cm are required to cover the office floor, excluding the area underneath the filing cabinet? The base of the filing cabinet is 1.25 m by 80 cm.

A 568   B 546   C 548   D 136.5   E 188   F 176.5

Answer: [   ]

29. The budget approved for organizing a seminar is £3,700. 35 per cent is spent on hiring a venue. 1/4 of the remainder is used to pay a speaker, while 2/3 is paid for transport to and from the venue. How much of the budget is left for refreshments? Round your answer to the nearest pound.

A £199   B £217   C £170   D £153   E £200   F £76

Answer: [   ]

Data interpretation

This type of test comprises tables or charts of information which you must interpret in order to answer the questions that follow. Thirty-four examples are provided.

Table 2.1   Acceptances for settlement in the UK: by category of acceptance

	Thousands			
	1985	1990	1995	2000
New Commonwealth				
Own right	4.1	2.4	1.7	1.6
Husbands	3.2	3.2	6.3	6.0
Wives	10.0	3.9	9.6	9.6
Children	10.7	3.2	4.5	4.5
Others	3.4	3.3	5.8	6.1
Total New Commonwealth	31.4	16.0	27.9	27.8
Rest of the World				
Own right	11.6	6.6	9.3	4.0
Husbands	3.4	6.1	5.4	4.9
Wives	6.8	4.8	3.7	9.0
Children	3.7	2.9	3.1	3.9
Others	2.3	3.6	4.7	3.2
Total Rest of the World	27.8	24.0	26.2	25.0
Total Acceptances	59.2	40.0	54.1	52.6

1.   How many people settled in the UK in 2000?

    A   25,000
    B   27,000
    C   48,000
    D   52,600
    E   54,000
    F   59,200

Answer: [ ]

2. In which year were acceptances from the New
    Commonwealth proportionally less than from the Rest of
    the World?

    A   1985
    B   1990
    C   1995
    D   2000
    E   None
    F   Information not available

    Answer: [   ]

3. In 1995 which category was the least accepted overall?

    A   Own right
    B   Husbands
    C   Wives
    D   Children
    E   Others
    F   None

    Answer: [   ]

4. How many more children from the Rest of the World were
    accepted in 2000 than in 1985?

    A   0
    B   2.0 thousand
    C   200
    D   800
    E   2000
    F   8000

    Answer: [   ]

5.   What percentage of total acceptances in 1990 were from the New Commonwealth?

A   20%
B   40%
C   60%
D   70%
E   80%
F   90%

Answer: [   ]

Table 2.2   All aboard the ferry: Summer 2002 Timetable*

Pier Head depart	Seaway arrive/depart	Riverside arrive/depart	Pier Head arrive	Fare £
10.00 am	10.30 am	10.40 am	10.50 am	2.20
11.00 am	11.30 am	11.40 am	11.50 am	2.20
12.00 pm	12.30 pm	12.40 pm	12.50 pm	2.20
1.00 pm	1.30 pm	1.40 pm	1.50 pm	2.20
2.00 pm	2.30 pm	2.40 pm	2.50 pm	2.20
3.00 pm	3.30 pm	3.40 pm	3.50 pm	2.20
4.15 pm	4.25 pm	4.35 pm	4.45 pm	1.15
4.45 pm	4.55 pm	5.05 pm	5.15 pm	1.15
5.15 pm	5.25 pm	5.35 pm	5.45 pm	1.15
5.45 pm	5.55 pm	6.05 pm	6.15 pm	1.15

*Between 10.00 am and 3.00 pm the ferry makes a scenic round trip, leaving Pier Head each hour on the hour

6.   How long is the scenic cruise?

A   30 minutes
B   50 minutes
C   1 hour
D   5 hours 50 minutes
E   6 hours
F   6 hours 15 minutes

Answer: [   ]

7.   What time does the 1.00 pm ferry from Pier Head arrive at
     Riverside?

   A   1.30 pm
   B   1.40 pm
   C   1.50 pm
   D   2.00 pm
   E   2.40 pm
   F   3.00 pm

                     Answer: [   ]

8.   What is the longest time the ferry waits at Pier Head?

   A   5 minutes
   B   10 minutes
   C   15 minutes
   D   20 minutes
   E   25 minutes
   F   30 minutes

                     Answer: [   ]

9.   A party of 50 tourists board the 2.00 pm scenic cruise.
     How much in total do they pay for this tour?

   A   £57.50
   B   £65.00
   C   £100.00
   D   £110.00
   E   £125.00
   F   £140.00

                     Answer: [   ]

10. At 4.00 pm a tanker anchors off Seaway. This results in a 15 minute delay between Seaway and Riverside on all journeys from then on. What time does the ferry finally finish at Pier Head that day?

A   5.00 pm
B   5.15 pm
C   6.15 pm
D   6.45 pm
E   7.15 pm
F   Insufficient information

Answer: [   ]

Delilah Smythe is baking cakes, but she has a gas oven and the recipe only gives temperatures in °C. She therefore looks up her handy conversion table:

Table 2.3   Conversion table

| Gas mark | Oven temperatures | |
	°F	°C
1	275	140
2	300	150
3	325	170
4	350	180
5	375	190
6	400	200
7	425	220
8	450	230
9	475	240

11. The recipe says bake the cakes at 180°C for 20–25 minutes until brown on top. What Gas Mark should Delilah use?

A 1
B 2
C 3
D 4
E 5
F 6

Answer: [   ]

12. At Gas Marks 2 and 6, what is the magnitude of °F to °C?

A x1
B x2
C x3
D x4
E x5
F x6

Answer: [   ]

13. What is the range in temperature, measured in °F, between Gas Marks 3 and 9?

A 70°F
B 100°F
C 125°F
D 150°F
E 175°F
F 200°F

Answer: [   ]

14. Delilah uses a thermometer to check the temperature of her oven at the various Gas Marks and finds that Gas Mark 6 is 5 per cent higher than it should be. What temperature, in °C, does the thermometer read?

    A 190°C
    B 200°C
    C 210°C
    D 220°C
    E 230°C
    F 240°C

Answer: [   ]

The Stephenson family love to shop. The family of five easily spends over £300 each week at Sainsways on groceries. The following is part of their till receipt for one week in March:

CUCUMBER WHOLE	0.59	g
ORGANIC ORANGES	1.49	g
S GREENS	0.75	g
S P/NUT/BUT SMTH	1.99	
S P/NUT/BUT SMTH	1.99	
* MULTISAVE *	−1.99	
S SATSUMA LARGE	1.79	g
PURE ORANGE JUICEX1LTR	0.99	
S SOAP MULTIPACK	1.75	
S SATSUMA LARGE	1.79	g
* MULTISAVE *	−1.79	
S TOOTHPASTE	0.88	
0.745 kg @ £2.49 / kg		
S GRAPES WHT S/LESS	1.86	g
**** TOT	302.60	
16/03/02 16.07		

Figure 2.1 Till receipt

15. How much is 1 litre of Pure Orange Juice?

    A £0.99
    B £1.49
    C £1.75
    D £1.79
    E £1.99
    F Information not supplied

Answer: [   ]

16. How much have the Stephenson family saved on multi-saves?

    A £1.79
    B £1.99
    C £2.67
    D £3.78
    E £4.02
    F £4.52

Answer: [   ]

17. How much did the Stephenson family spend on groceries (g)?

    A £0.56
    B £1.42
    C £3.65
    D £5.64
    E £6.48
    F £8.27

Answer: [   ]

18. Mrs Stephenson has collected 250 discount points on her loyalty card, worth 10 per cent of the total bill. How much does she save?

   A   £20.50
   B   £25.00
   C   £30.26
   D   £33.60
   E   £40.62
   F   £40.88

Answer: [   ]

Table 2.4   Holiday entitlement

Name	Annual holiday entitlement	Carry-over from the previous year	Total numbers of days taken to date	Days remaining
M Adams	23	0	1.5	18.5
S Brown	23	−1	11	?
H Evans	27	2	5	?
H Hasan	26	0	5	?
A Milic	23	−1.5	8	?

19. From the table above, how many more days holiday can S Brown take in the current year?

   A 22   B 24   C 11   D 21 E 19   F 18

Answer: [   ]

20. Employees are given 23 days holiday per year for the first two years of service and then half a day for every six months. How many years has H Hasan been with the company?

   A 4   B 6   C 4.5   D 5   E 3.5   F 5.5

Answer: [   ]

21. If A Milic earns £300 per week and decides to resign and work throughout her notice period without taking any more holiday days, how much holiday pay will she be entitled to? Assume that her last day of employment coincides with the end of the year for holiday entitlement purposes.

A £900 B £22.22 C £810 D £620 E £720 F £600

Answer: [   ]

22. If S Brown wants to go away for 15 days, how many days unpaid leave should he take in addition to his holiday entitlement?

A 5 B 3 C 0 D 1 E 4 F 2

Answer: [   ]

Table 2.5 shows the realized sales of a mobile phone package priced at £49, and a commission earned per sale.

Table 2.5   Mobile phone package sales

Name	Target in units	Units sold	Commission %	Total %	Earnings
S Amed	25	24	3	35.28	
B Fay	25	31	3	?	
S Grant	25	28	3	41.16	
I Jones	25	21	3	30.87	
O Khann	25	26	3	38.22	
A Lewis	25	26	3	38.22	

23. From the table calculate the total commission earned by B Fay.

A £28.30   B £93.00   C £45.57   D £36.75   E £55.75
F £28.00

Answer: [　　　　　　　　]

24. On average, how many units did each salesperson sell during the period?

A 26   B 22   C 21   D 29   E 27   F 28

Answer: [　　　　　　　　]

25. If the company decided to increase the commission to 5 per cent for every unit sold above the target, how much commission would S Grant earn?

A £52.30   B £60   C £37.75   D £53.17   E £44.10
F £43.17

Answer: [　　　　　　　　]

26. What percentage of employees reached the target?

A 25%   B 30%   C 60%   D 70%   E 66.6%   F 33.3%

Answer: [　　　　　　　　]

Table 2.6 shows the net total (income after tax) generated by the products.

Table 2.6   Net total

Product	Number of units in 000s	Cost of raw material per unit £	Manufacturing cost per unit £	Total cost per unit £	Sales price per unit £	Total sales revenue £ (sales price − total cost x number of units)
A	21.5	3.75	2	5.75	7.5	37,625.00
B	18	2.19	3.17	5.36	6.25	1,602.00
C	7	8.70	4.2	12.90	13.4	3,500.00
D	11.75	0.57	4.8	5.37	7.99	?
E	12.8	1.18	0.27	1.45	4.5	39,040.00
F	9.25	4.3	1.5	5.8	6.25	4,162.50
Total	80.3	20.69	15.94	36.63	45.89	743,578.00
Profit (−23%)						?

27. From the table calculate which product is the most profitable.

    A F   B D   C E   D A   E C   F B

    Answer: [   ]

28. If the manufacturing cost were reduced by 50 per cent, what would be the total sales revenue for product A?

    A £60,700 B £49,125 C £57,755 D £59,125
    E £48,950 F £66,789

    Answer: [   ]

29. Calculate the total sales revenue for product D.

    A £40,500 B £30,785 C £30,885 D £45,125
    E £33,600 F £30,780

    Answer: [   ]

30. Assuming that the tax is 23 per cent, calculate the total profit for the period.

   A £572,555.06   B £57,255.56   C £171,022.94
   D £17,122.94   E £743,250.00   F £74,325.00

   Answer: [   ]

Table 2.7

Year	1st quarter average temperature in °C	2nd quarter average temperature in °C	3rd quarter average temperature in °C	4th quarter average temperature in °C
1996	1	12.5	23	2
1997	2	11	22	4
1998	−1	13.5	24	3.5
1999	0	10	21.5	4
2000	1.5	15.5	23	2
2001	2	14.5	25	?

31. From Table 2.7, what was the average temperature in the year 1999?

   A 8.9°C   B 9°C   C 8.8°C   D 11.8°C   E 11.7°C
   F 10.7°C

   Answer: [   ]

32. Calculate the net change in temperature between the first and fourth quarters for the year 1998.

   A 2.5°C   B 4.5C°   C 3.5°C   D 2.5°C   E −4°C
   F −4.5°C

   Answer: [   ]

33. In what year was the greatest change in temperature noted
     between the first and third quarters?

     A 1996   B 1997   C 1998   D 1999   E 2000   F 2001

     Answer: [   ]

34. If the average temperature in the year 2000 was the same
     as in 2001, what was the temperature in the final quarter
     in 2001?

     A 2   B 2.5   C 1.5   D 1   E 5   F 0.5

     Answer: [   ]

Word swap

Each question comprises a sentence in which two words need to
be interchanged to make it read sensibly. Only swap two words
so that one replaces the other. This means that one word must
be placed where you have taken the other. Try the following 19
examples.

1.   A loss of muscle movement is accompanied by rapid tone
     of the eyes.

     Answer: [   ]

2.   Sometimes these remedies can result remarkably quickly,
     with a positive work occurring in a matter of hours.

     Answer: [   ]

3.   Completely safe, it is made from artificial ingredients, with
     no natural colours, flavours or preservatives.

     Answer: [   ]

4. Over the centuries and of these properties have been sold some other properties purchased.

   Answer: [   ]

5. Only the small doorway in the remain on the ground floor and a similar doorway on the northern wall of the gallery recess today.

   Answer: [   ]

6. They take most day as it comes and work very hard to make the each of it.

   Answer: [   ]

7. Perhaps the greatest advantage to the constant ability is see two sides to every story.

   Answer: [   ]

8. It's true they have an enthusiastic style for information and a bubbly hunger of expression.

   Answer: [   ]

9. The national minimum wage is over £4.20 an hour for workers aged 22 years or now.

   Answer: [   ]

10. How thrilling to camp out in the jungle surrounded of the incredible sounds by the equatorial night.

    Answer: [   ]

11. Many people believe that we should eat our national produce more and only respect fruit and vegetables that are in season.

Answer: [   ]

12. If your dog does kill a rabbit it may be necessary for you to put the rabbit out of any misery and catch it yourself.

Answer: [   ]

13. A few golfers rake to forget the sand in the bunker after their shot which can cause problems for the next person.

Answer: [   ]

14. The most popular numerous orange is the Seville, a thinned-skinned orange-red fruit, with acid deep yellow flesh and bitter pips.

Answer: [   ]

15. The adaptable alphabet is the most highly developed, convenient and the most easily Roman system of writing.

Answer: [   ]

16. A damp-proof course is a layer of inserted material impervious in the bottom of a house wall about 20 cm above ground level.

Answer: [   ]

17. There are few things as idyllic as opening up the picnic basket in an irritating spot only to find the tin/bottle opener is back on the kitchen table.

Answer: [   ]

18. The known benefits of raw fish, soya beans and green tea have long been health to the Japanese.

Answer: [   ]

19. It would be unwise to venture out of the house during springtime in England about an umbrella without one's person.

Answer: [   ]

Missing words

Each group of two words is in the order in which they fall in the sentence. It is your task to identify which are the correct pairings from the sound or look-alike alternatives. Underline the correct pair. Try the following 21 examples.

1. To _____ any sort of change the community must feel the _____ of the proposed legislation.

affect	effect	aphect	ephect
effect	effect	ephect	aphect

2. He was _____ upon the goodwill of his father; he was after all his sole _____.

depandent	dependant	dependent	deapendent
depandant	dependent	dependant	deapandant

3. He _____ with pleasure his _____ to fish in the Loch.

excepted	accepted	excepted	accepted
license	licence	licence	license

4. It will be on David's _____ if Lucy does not remain
    _____ throughout the night.

    | concience | conscience | conscience | concience |
    | conscious | conscious | consious | conscious |

5. The girl _____ a glass out of the _____ window.

    | threw | through | threw | though |
    | rear | rare | reer | wrear |

6. The cutter he was going to use to _____ the tree had a
    blueish _____ to it.

    | hugh | hew | hue | huw |
    | hue | hue | hew | hugh |

7. Honesty was Helen's first _____ when she became
    _____ of the school.

    | princepal | princaple | principle | principal |
    | princaple | principle | principal | princepal |

8. It is common _____ to _____ to the Queen as she
    passes.

    | courtesy | curtesy | courtesey | curtesey |
    | curtsy | quertsey | courtsey | qurtsey |

9. The raid on the _____ resulted in _____ action
    being taken.

    | dispensery | dispansary | disspensary | disspensery |
    | disciplinery | disciplinary | disiplinary | disiplinery |

10. She kept a _____ of artefacts for when the _____ of
    pilgrims came by.

    | horde | hord | hoard | whord |
    | hoarde | herd | horde | wherd |

11. What you can do to make your cut _____ last even longer is to dip the cut ends in _____ before putting in water.

| flours | fluers | flowers | flouers |
| flower | flouer | flour | fluer |

12. Take a _____ of fruit and _____ the skin with a pin.

| peice | piece | peace | piece |
| pearce | peirce | peirse | pierce |

13. I had to _____ the authorities she was too _____ to travel.

| informe | inform | infourm | informn |
| inferm | infirm | inferme | infirmn |

14. It was the _____ of such a musician to _____ for five hours each day.

| practise | practice | practisce | practicse |
| practice | practise | practicse | practisce |

15. It was while the van was _____ at the traffic lights that the _____ on board was stolen.

| stationary | stationery | stationray | stationarey |
| stationery | stationary | stationrey | stationeray |

16. On the back of the _____ was a _____ for marmalade.

| rescite | resept | reciept | receipt |
| resepy | recipy | receipe | recipe |

17. For the best results you must do the _____ _____ upon getting up.

| excersises | exersises | excercises | exercises |
| imediately | immidiately | immedietely | immediately |

18. As a _____ you are not allowed to _____ the machine.

miner	minor	miener	mienor
opporate	operate	oparate	operate

19. These _____ took those other _____ books by mistake.

boys	bouys	boy's	boys'
boys'	bouy's	boys	boy's

20. _____ most unusual for the dog to refuse _____ bone like that.

its	it's	its'	it
it's	its	it	its'

21. Even when using a _____ line the wall does not look _____.

plum	plumb	plump	plumn
strait	straight	strate	streight

Correct sentence

Identify which of the options is correct in terms of grammar, spelling and punctuation. Below you will find 20 examples of this type of question. Underline the correct sentence.

1. a) If you're looking for an evening out this month, there are big offers on musicals and pop concerts.
    b) If you're looking for an evening out this month, there is big offers on musicals and pop concerts.
    c) If your looking for an evening out this month, there are big offers on musicals and pop concerts.
    d) None of these.

2. a) The consumer is protected from exploitation by a given seller by the existence of other seller's he can buy from.
    b) The consumer is protected from exploitation by a given seller by the existence of other sellers from whom he can buy.
    c) The consumer are protected from exploitation by a given seller by the existence of other sellers from whom he can buy.
    d) None of these.

3. a) All mammal's produce eggs within which their young develop.
    b) All mammal's produce eggs which their young develop in.
    c) All mammals produce eggs within which their young develop.
    d) None of these.

4. a) There are maps and travel books available for most of England's towns and cities.
    b) There is maps and travel books available for most of England's towns and cities.
    c) Maps and travel books is available for most of England's Towns and Cities.
    d) None of these.

5. a) Further information will be given to you when you visited the head office.
    b) Further information was given to you when you visit the head office.
    c) Further information will be given to you when you visit the head office.
    d) None of these.

6. a) She married again, which surprised everybody who knew her.
    b) She married again, what surprised everybody who knew her.

    c) She married again, that surprised everybody whom knew her.

    d) None of these.

7. a) There are a wide selection of gifts available, all of which can be ordered by post or online.

    b) There is a wide selection of gifts available, all of which can be ordered by post online.

    c) There is a wide selection of gifts available, all of which will be ordered by post or online.

    d) None of these.

8. a) At that moment, I wished I had gone to the same university as John.

    b) At that moment, I wished I was gone to the same university as John.

    c) At that moment, I wished I had gone to the same university as John did.

    d) None of these.

9. a) When I go to university I'll not have no time for reading novels.

    b) When I go to university I won't have no time for reading novels.

    c) When I go to university I will have no time for reading novels.

    d) None of these.

10. a) The coach was expecting great things off the team this season.

    b) The coach was expecting great things of the team this season.

    c) The coach were expecting great things of the team this season.

    d) None of these.

11. a)　Whenever a new book comes out they are the first to buy a copy.
　　b)　Whenever a new book comes out they was the first to buy a copy.
　　c)　Whenever a new book comes out they are the first too buy a copy.
　　d)　None of these.

12. a)　There are the promise of a more secure future for those who save on a regular basis.
　　b)　There is the promise of a more secure future for those who save on a regular basis.
　　c)　There is the promise of a more secure future for those who saved on a regular basis.
　　d)　None of these.

13. a)　If the customer does return the goods, you must check them before you gave a refund.
　　b)　If the customer did return the goods, you must ensure you check them before giving a refund.
　　c)　If the customer should return the goods, you must ensure you check them before giving a refund.
　　d)　None of the above.

14. a)　There's places where that kind of behaviour is unacceptable.
　　b)　There are places where that kind of behaviour is unacceptable.
　　c)　There's place's where that kind of behaviour is unacceptable.
　　d)　None of these.

15. a)　This borough is very good about providing bins for recycling metal, plastic, glass and paper.
　　b)　This borough are very good about providing bins for recycling metal, plastic, glass and paper.

c) This borough is very good while providing bins for recycling metal, plastic, glass and paper.

d) None of these.

16. a) One of the most important notes on the piano are
    Middle C.

b) One of the most important note's on the piano is Middle
   C.

c) One of the most important notes on the piano is Middle
   C.

d) None of these.

17. a) Once Simon got angry it takes a long while for him to
    calm down.

b) Once Simon gets angry it takes a long while for him to
   calm down.

c) Once Simon gets angry it took a long while for him to
   calm down.

d) None of these.

18. a) We pitched our tent on the bank of the river Stour, near
    where it joins the Avon.

b) We pitched our tent on the bank of the river Stour, near
   where it joined the Avon.

c) We pitched our tent on the bank of the river Stour, near
   where it is joining the Avon.

d) None of these.

19. a) They was walking along the beach all day yesterday and
    they will be walking along the cliff all day tomorrow.

b) They were walking along the beach all day yesterday
   and they were walking along the cliff all day tomorrow.

c) They were walking along the beach all day yesterday
   and they will be walking along the cliff all day
   tomorrow.

d) None of these.

20. a) It was Galileo who discovered that Jupiter has moons.
    b) It was Galileo whom discovered that Jupiter had moons.
    c) It's Galileo who discovered that Jupiter had moons.
    d) None of these.

3

Clerical Mock Tests

Mock test 1

Quantitative reasoning

This test comprises 30 questions. Allow yourself 20 minutes to complete it.

1. A secretary is posting 11 letters to clients. She is sending seven letters by first class post at 27p per letter. The remaining four letters she is sending by second class post at 19p per letter. How much postage is being paid for all 11 letters?

    A £2.77   B £1.27   C £1.76   D £2.41   E £2.56   F £2.65

    Answer: [   ]

2. A delivery was due to arrive at 14.45 but was 27 minutes late. What time did it arrive?

    A 15.07   B 15.05   C 15.22   D 15.12   E 15.42   F 15.02

    Answer: [   ]

3. Ann deposits £1,000.00 in her savings account. The interest rate on her savings is 5 per cent. How long is it before Ann has earned £157 of interest?

    A 2.5 years   B 3.5 years   C 4 years   D 1.5 years
    E 1 year   F 3 years

    Answer: [   ]

4. A company purchased a new PC for £800. The depreciation rate (decrease in value) is 40 per cent for the first year and 25 per cent of the depreciated sum for every following year. What is the value of the PC at the end of the third year?

    A £48   B £240   C £270   D £280   E £230   F £58

    Answer: [   ]

5. An office junior can type 30 wpm. If he types steadily for 30 minutes how many words will he type?

    A 90   B 600   C 60   D 120   E 800   F 900

    Answer: [   ]

6. An accountant has worked for a company for four months. His holiday allowance is 1.25 days per month in service. How many holiday days is the accountant entitled to after four months' service?

A 4.25 days   B 6 days   C 5.5 days   D 3 days   E 5 days F 2 days

Answer: [   ]

7. Petra is ordering stationery. All the prices are shown before VAT (17.5 per cent). If Petra orders two boxes of staples for £1.75 each and five large notebooks for £1.15 each, how much will the total be including the VAT?

A £10.45   B £9.45   C £9.75   D £10.87   E £11.75 F £9.45

Answer: [   ]

8. A company manufactures small, medium and large buttons at the ratio of 1:5:3. If in the year 2001 the total of buttons manufactured was 18,900, how many of them were large?

A 2,100   B 6,300   C 10,500   D 1,300   E 13,600 F 6,800

Answer: [   ]

9. A parcel weighing 1 kg costs £3.50 to post. If prices are proportional to weight, how much would it cost to post a parcel that weighs 200 gm?

A £1.75   B £1.25   C £0.75   D £0.70   E £1.15   F £0.89

Answer: [   ]

10. A meeting is scheduled to start at 2:45 pm and last for 1h 30 min. The trip from the office to the meeting venue takes 45 min. If Barbara is to attend the meeting, how long will she be away from the office?

    A 3 h B 2 h 45 min C 3 h 15 min D 4 h E 2 h 30 min
    F 3 h 45 min

    Answer: [ ]

11. A company decides to buy corporate membership for its employees at the local gym. The gym is offering 20 per cent discount on all corporate memberships. How many members of staff should join for the company to receive the equivalent of two memberships for free?

    A 5 B 12 C 8 D 10 E 20 F 15

    Answer: [ ]

12. With an offer buy-one-get-one-free, what percentage is saved?

    A 25% B 33% C 50% D 20% E 35% F 75%

    Answer: [ ]

13. The total postage cost for two parcels of different weight is £3.40. If the weight ratio is 2 : 2.3, calculate the postage for the heavier parcel.

    A £1.57 B £2.10 C £1.82 D £1.90 E £2.18 F £2.40

    Answer: [ ]

14. Attendee A and attendee B are arriving for the same meeting from different locations. Attendee A is travelling at 47 mph over the distance of 38 miles. Attendee B is

travelling at 38 mph over 29 miles. If they start their journeys at the same time, what will be the time gap between their arrivals? Round your answer up to a full minute.

A 5 mins   B 3 mins   C 2 mins   D 7 mins   E 8 mins
F 4 mins

Answer: [   ]

15. If 3 per cent of the price is £24, how much is the full price?

A £600   B £240   C £750   D £850   E £400   F £800

Answer: [   ]

16. A company is running a special promotion and is discounting its product by 25 per cent. If the price before the discount was £10 and the total revenue was £1,000, by what percentage should sales increase to generate the same amount of revenue as before the reduction?

A 7.5%   B 25%   C 10%   D 33.3%   E 12.5%   F 15%

Answer: [   ]

17. If a package contains four boxes of staples and each consecutive box is 50 per cent heavier than the previous one, how heavy is the heaviest box if the total weight of a package is 1 kg? Round your answer up to the nearest gram.

A 500 gm   B 300 gm   C 450 gm   D 685 gm   E 416 gm
F 725 gm

Answer: [   ]

18. Sales staff A and B are selling the same product. A sold £1,000.00 worth of products and received 3.5 per cent commission, while B received only 3 per cent. How many more sales should B realize to achieve the same amount of commission as A?

    A 0.5% more   B 50% more   C 16.66% more
    D 25% more   E 10.55% more   F 12.77% more

    Answer:

19. A videoconference is to take place between Dubai, London and New York. If Dubai is four hours behind London and New York is six hours ahead of London, and if the conference is to start at 2.30 pm 11 Jan 02 New York time, what time will it start in Dubai?

    A 00.30 am 10 Jan 02   B 02.30 am 10 Jan 02
    C 00.30 am 11 Jan 02   D 02.30 am 11 Jan 02
    E 04.30 am 11 Jan 02   F 02.30 am 12 Jan 02

    Answer:

20. 20 per cent of office workers travel to work by car, 70 per cent travel by train and 10 per cent travel by bus. Express these values as a ratio.

    A 2:3.5:1   B 1:1.6:2   C 2:2.5:1   D 2:2.5:1.5   E 1.5:2.5:1
    F 1:3.5:0.5

    Answer:

21. Express 3/20 as a percentage.

    A 10%   B 20%   C 13.5%   D 15%   E 22.5%   F 35%

    Answer:

22. One metre of optical fibre cable is priced at £7.99. Calculate the price of one foot of cable considering that 1 ft = 0.305 m.

    A £4.50   B £7.68   C £2.99   D £3.99   E £2.25   F £2.44

    Answer: [   ]

23. The maximum weight allowed in the office elevator is 225 kg. What is the maximum weight allowed expressed in lbs, if 1 lb = 0.45 kg?

    A 499.50 lb   B 500.00 lb   C 101.25 lb   D 370.00 lb
    E 350.00 lb   F 325.00 lb

    Answer: [   ]

24. If a vehicle travels at 35 mph, how many kilometres would it travel in 30 min? 1 km = 0.621 miles

    A 33 km   B 56 km   C 28 km   D 66 km   E 18 km
    F 17.5 km

    Answer: [   ]

25. Kim usually flies from Heathrow, and her taxi fare to the airport is on average £12 for a 25 min drive. This time, however, Kim is flying from Luton and the taxi drive will take 45 min. Assuming taxi fares are proportionate to the time taken, how much should Kim expect to pay for her drive to Luton airport?

    A £15.60   B £16.20   C £21.60   D £20.60   E £12.60
    F £6.20

    Answer: [   ]

26. The price of laminated flooring is £6.25 per sq ft. How much would it cost to buy enough flooring to cover 5 sq m if 1 ft = 0.305 m? Calculate the answer to the nearest pound.

    A £314   B £150   C £218   D £298   E £336   F £170

    Answer:

27. Frank takes pride in achieving an average of 35 mph during his journey to work of 25 miles. However, in the evening his same journey home takes twice as long. What is Frank's daily average speed?

    A 15.25 mph   B 25.25 mph   C 18.25 mph   D 26.25 mph
    E 30.25 mph   F 20.25 mph

    Answer:

28. In January a project team spent 50 per cent of its total budget plus £1,000. In February 50 per cent of the remainder was spent plus a further £1,000. If in March the project team still had £5,000 of the budgeted amount at its disposal, how much was the total budget assigned?

    A £25,000   B £26,000   C £16,000   D £17,500
    E £24,000   F £15,000

    Answer:

29. A shelf in a storage room is 1.83 m wide. How many files can be stored if the width of a single file is 1 inch? 1 inch = 0.083 ft; 1 ft = 0.305 m.

    A 6   B 12   C 60   D 84   E 70   F 72

    Answer:

30. Marie leaves her house at 7.30 am to arrive at the office at 9 am. If the distance between Marie's house and the office is 56 miles and if she takes a 20 minute break halfway, what is the average speed Marie should drive to arrive on time?

A 45 mph   B 48 mph   C 58 mph   D 37.8 mph
E 43 mph   F 27.5 mph

Answer: [   ]

End of test.

Mock test 2

Data interpretation

This test comprises 24 questions. Allow yourself 20 minutes to complete it.

Table 3.1   Market research findings on the preferred colour of pre-paid vouchers

Total no. of Interviewees	Age group	Positive responses by preferred colour			
		Green	Blue	Pink	Red
200	15–25	58	45	33	64
200	26–35	68	53	40	39
300	36–45	42	93	70	95
160	46–55	48	62	16	40
90	56–65	25	18	30	17
50	66–75	11	15	10	14

1. Which age group most favoured the green pre-paid vouchers?

    A 15–25   B 26–35   C 36–45   D 46–55   E 56–65
    F 66–75

    Answer: [   ]

2. How many interviewees most favoured the red vouchers?

    A 113   B 325   C 244   D 269   E 332   F 543

    Answer: [   ]

3. What percentage of 15–25-year-olds favoured the pink vouchers?

    A 12%   B 17.5%   C 22%   D 16.5%   E 66.66%
    F 33.33%

    Answer: [   ]

4. Which age group gave the proportionally smallest percentage response to green vouchers?

    A 15–25   B 26–35   C 36–45   D 46–55   E 56–65
    F 66–75

    Answer: [   ]

Table 3.2 shows the current currency exchange rate into pounds Sterling. The commission charged per transaction is 4.5 per cent.

Table 3.2   Currency exchange rate into pounds Sterling

Country	Currency	Selling Price	Buying Price	Remarks
Australia	Dollar	2.79	2.99	—
Turkey	Lira	—	24.49	—
South Africa	Rand	3.18	3.38	—
Israel	Shekel	—	591.86	500 and above
New Zealand	Dollar	5.76	6.18	10 and above
*	Euro	1.55	1.66	—

5. Claire went to South Africa and returned with 280 Rand unspent. How much will she get if she sells them at the current rate, before commission?

    A £82.67 B £75.55 C £79.11 D £82.84 E £88.05
    F £84.08

    Answer:

6. A company is sending its executives on a business trip to Australia, and the total cash allowance is £1,750.00. How many Australian dollars can be purchased after the commission?

    A 580.78 B 4,997.03 C 5,019.88 D 5,102.21
    E 5,467.96 F 599.01

    Answer:

7. The same trip (as in question 6) was cancelled at the last minute, so the company decided to change the unneeded Australian dollars back into pounds. How much in £ sterling did it receive?

A £1,750.00 B £1,791.05 C £13,314.00 D £1,596.04
E £1,710.45 F £4,997.03

Answer:

8. Take the average exchange of the selling and buying price for the euro and use it to calculate 0.5 euro expressed in pounds.

A £0.31 B £0.62 C £0.27 D £0.95 E £0.25 F £0.81

Answer:

Table 3.3   Bank account holder records

Account holder	Initial balance £	Money deposited £	Money withdrawn £
S Davies	23.45	0	−20.00
H Gomez	227.50	50.00	−270.00
J K Josef	386.16	12.50	0
O McCormack	−250.00	360.00	−25.00
F Wild	−76.50	50.00	0
D Zair	36.00	6.00	−40.00

9. From Table 3.3, what percentage of account holders are overdrawn?

A 15% B 33.33% C 19% D 16.66% E 24.5%
F 17.5%

Answer:

10. If F Wild deposits £2 every fortnight, makes no more withdrawals and is charged no interest or fees, how many weeks before his overdraft is paid off in full?

    A 13.2   B 53   C 6.6   D 12.3   E 25.6   F 26.5

    Answer: [   ]

11. If S Davis's salary of £800 is deposited on 4 February and her rent of £95 is debited on the same day, what will her balance be on 5 February?

    A £750.00   B £709.45   C £708.45   D £705.00
    E £728.50   F £748.00

    Answer: [   ]

12. What is O McCormack's final balance?

    A £85.00   B £155.00   C £135.00   D £90.00   E £45.00
    F £68.00

    Answer: [   ]

13. A first class letter to Aberdeen weights 550 g and a letter to France weights 12 g. According to Table 3.4, how much is the total postage?

    A £2.03   B £2.55   C £2.88   D £2.50   E £3.00   F £3.88

    Answer: [   ]

14. A first class letter to Dover weights 0.96 kg. How much is the total postage?

    A £3.36   B £2.51   C £3.15   D £2.15   E £2.36   F £3.51

    Answer: [   ]

Table 3.4 Postage

UK	Weight up to:	60g	100g	150g	200g	300g	400g	500g	Each +250
	First class £	0.27	0.41	0.57	0.72	0.96	1.30	1.66	0.85
	Second class £	0.19	0.33	0.44	0.54	0.76	1.05	—	—
Worldwide	Weight up to:	10g	20g	40g	60g	80g	100g	Each + 50g	
	Europe	x	0.37	0.52	0.68	0.84	0.99	0.59	
	W Zone 1	0.47	0.68	1.05	1.42	1.79	2.16	1.25	
	W Zone 2	0.47	0.68	1.12	1.56	2.00	2.44	1.40	

15. A letter to Europe is three and a half times lighter than a 350 g letter to the UK, posted first class. How much would it cost to post both letters?

    A £1.95   B £4.30   C £2.12   D £3.50   E £3.29   F £2.29

    Answer: [ ]

16. A first letter to W Zone 1 weighs 40 g, and a second letter to the same destination weighs 65 g. What would the difference in price be if the letters were sent together as a single letter or separately?

    A £1.18   B £1.23   C £0.26   D £0.47   E £0.57   F £0.95

    Answer: [ ]

Table 3.5   Mortality rates

2001	Population in millions	Births per thousand	Deaths per thousand
Germany	83	9.15	9.2
France	60	12	9
Italy	58	9.05	10.05
Spain	40	9.25	9.15
England	60	11.54	10.35
Holland	16	8.69	7.85

17. From Table 3.5, what was the total number of deaths in Germany during the year?

A 9,200   B 763,600   C 92,000   D 76,300   E 7,630
F 184,000

Answer:

18. What was the total increase in population in France?

A 720,000   B 180,000   C 300,000   D 18,000   E 72,000
F 640,000

Answer:

19. If the population growth per year remains the same, what would the total French population be at the end of 2002?

A 60,360,000   B 60,000,360   C 60,360,540
D 60,366,000   E 63,600,000   F 63,654,000

Answer:

20. Which countries are experiencing a decrease in population?

A France & England   B England & Germany   C Spain & Italy   D Holland & Spain   E Italy & Germany
F Germany & France

Answer:

Table 3.6

2001	Total area sq km	Land	Water	Arable land, permanent pastures and woodland %
Germany	357,021	349,223	7,798	33
France	547,030	545,630	1,400	33
Italy	301,230	294,020	7,210	31
Spain	504,782	499,542	5,240	30
England	244,820	241,590	3,230	25
Holland	41,526	33,883	7,643	25

21. From Table 3.6, how many sq km of land are there in France if you exclude the arable land, permanent pasture and woodlands?

    A 113,810 sq km   B 192,700 sq km   C 366,510 sq km
    D 180,058 sq km   E 118,410 sq km   F 365,572 sq km

    Answer: [   ]

22. What is the total area of Holland expressed in sq miles? 1 m = 1.6 km. Round your answer to the nearest sq mile.

    A 19,125 sq m   B 27,750 sq m   C 16,195 sq m
    D 27,075 sq m   E 27,065 sq m   F 18,195 sq m

    Answer: [   ]

23. What percentage of Holland's total territory is covered by water?

    A 17%   B 0.17%   C 1.3%   D 12.3%   E 9.5%
    F 18.4%

    Answer: [   ]

24. How many sq km of total Spanish territory is covered by arable land, permanent pastures and woodland?

A 253,445.00 sq km   B 353,347.50 sq km
C 355,723.50 sq km   D 188,670.00 sq km
E 199,887.00 sq km   F 151,434.50 sq km

Answer: [   ]

End of test.

Mock test 3

Verbal reasoning

This test comprises 20 questions. Allow yourself 8 minutes to complete it.

Underline the words to be interchanged, or the pair that correctly completes the sentence.

1. Always remember when packing for travelling to half take the clothes and double the money.

2. The only equipment really needed in the kitchen is a couple of sharp pans and some stainless steel knives.

3. Only if your guest is on the name list will you be allowed in prior to the start of the show.

4. You must pass the actual test before you can take the written driving test.

5. It is quite untrue fact pigs are dirty, they are in that very clean animals.

6. The very strong traffic in winter often means the bridge has to be closed to winds.

7. Some spiders have an irrational fear of people, even very small ones.

8. One of the most important problems of an MP's job is meeting constituents and discussing their aspects.

9. Two parties who want to benefit with one another both communicate from coming to a common agreement about the words they use.

10. Keeping abreast of essential affairs is current for any modern writer.

11. At a rung hour of the evening, a bell was fixed signalling that all fires were to be extinguished.

12. All her _____ sat on the left side of the _____ in the church.

| guesseds | geusts | gests | guests |
| aile | isle | iasle | aisle |

13. The _____ was _____ to keep order in the barracks.

| sargent | sargeant | sergeant | sergent |
| recquired | recquird | required | reqired |

14. They were all _____ to another _____.

| transferred | transffered | transfferred | transfered |
| regiment | regement | regimant | regament |

15. He was made _____ _____ of his club.

| honary | honory | honorary | honorery |
| presidant | presedent | president | presedant |

16. You need to _____ away the _____ before using.

| pear | pare | pair | peir |
| exess | excess | exsess | ecsess |

17. The _____ of terror _____ to last for ever.

| reign | rain | rein | raign |
| seemed | seamed | seemd | seamd |

18. The ship docked at the _____ to allow passengers to _____.

| queye | quaye | quay | quey |
| borde | bord | board | boarde |

19. He had to pay by _____ _____ he did not have enough cash on him.

| check | cheque | checcque | checke |
| becawse | because | becuase | because |

20. I will _____ the same tomorrow as I _____ yesterday.

eate	ate	eat	eat
eaten	ated	ate	eated

End of test.

Mock test 4

Correct sentence

This test comprises 20 questions. Allow yourself 8 minutes to complete it.

Underline the correct sentence.

1. a) If she's only listened to me, this would never have happened.
    b) If she had only listened to me, this would never have happened.
    c) If she will only listen to me, this will never have happend.
    d) None of these.

2. a) There's just three thing's you need to know about Jack.
    b) There's just three things you need to know about Jack.
    c) There are just three things you need to know about Jack.
    d) None of these.

3. a) If I was you I'd see a doctor.
    b) If I were you I'd see a doctor.
    c) If I was you I'll see a doctor.
    d) None of these.

4. a) It looks like everyone has gone to the cinema.
    b) It looked like everyone has gone to the cinema.
    c) It looks like everyone had gone to the cinema.
    d) None of these.

5. a) Either Jane or her sister are bringing the dessert.
    b) Either Jane or her sister is bringing the dessert.
    c) Either Jane or her sister were bringing the dessert.
    d) None of these.

6. a) If I hadn't had my seatbelt on I'll be dead.
    b) If I didn't have my seatbelt on I'll have been dead.
    c) If I hadn't had my seatbelt on I would be dead.
    d) None of these.

7. a) From Thursday you cannot have either the blue nor the black pens.
    b) From Thursday you cannot have either the blue or the black pens.
    c) From Thursday you cannot have neither the blue nor the black pens.
    d) None of these.

8. a) I have been informed that neither Mandy nor Helen will be able to be there on Saturday.
    b) I have been informed that neither Mandy or Helen will be able to be there on Saturday.
    c) I have been informed that not either Mandy or Helen will be able to be there on Saturday.
    d) None of these.

9. a) Owning a dog is very different to owning a cat.
    b) Owning a dog is very different from owning a cat.
    c) Owning a dog is very different over owning a cat.
    d) None of these.

10. a) Compared with analogue TV, digital TV provides the consumer with a greater choice of programmes to watch.
    b) Compared to analogue TV, digital TV provides the consumer with a greater choice of programmes to watch.
    c) Compared to analogue TV, digital TV provided the consumer with a greater choice of programmes to watch.
    d) None of these.

11. a) If you was to go fishing at night you will find that you caught more fish than during the day.
    b) If you was to go fishing at night you might find that you catch more fish than during the day.
    c) If you were to go fishing at night you might find that you catch more fish than during the day.
    d) None of these.

12. a) Although the house and barn are on the same property, they will be sold separately.
    b) Although the house and barn were on the same property, they will be sold separately.
    c) Although the house and barn was on the same property, they were to be sold separately.
    d) None of these.

13. a) The school have insisted that no child leaves the playground until their parent arrives.
    b) The school has insisted that no child leaves the playground until their parent arrives.
    c) The school have insisted that no child leaves the playground until their parent arrived.
    d) None of these.

14. a) The Managing Director wanted you and I to attend the meeting.
    b) The Managing Director wanted you and me to attend the meeting.
    c) The Managing Director wanted me and you to attend the meeting.
    d) None of these.

15. a) Each night before I go to bed I made myself a cup of cocoa.
    b) Each night before I go to bed I make myself a cup of cocoa.

   c) Each night before I go to bed I makes myself a cup of cocoa.
   d) None of these.

16. a) Carol thought it an honour to receive an MBE.
    b) Carol thought it a honour to receive an MBE.
    c) Carol thought it an honour to receive a MBE.
    d) None of these.

17. a) It looks like it's going to rain.
    b) It looks like it's about to rain.
    c) It looks as if it is going to rain.
    d) None of these.

18. a) Every one of the new computers in the main office have been virus checked.
    b) Every one of the new computers in the main office has been virus checked.
    c) Every one of the new computers in the main office been virus checked.
    d) None of these.

19. a) It is equally important to check your credit card statement as it is your bank statement.
    b) It is equally as important to cheque your credit card statement as it is your bank statement.
    c) It is equally as important to check your credit card statement as it is your bank statement.
    d) None of these.

20. a) Mike seems to always do it that way.
    b) Mike seems to do it that way always.
    c) Mike always seems to do it that way.
    d) None of these

End of test.

Practice for the Fast Stream

The Fast Stream Qualifying Test comprises three tests and what is called a biodata questionnaire. The material in this and the next chapter is intended to provide practice material for the three tests only.

The Fast Stream Test is carefully explained in the booklet sent out to all candidates. It is vital that you study this document fully and ensure that you are totally familiar with the format and type of questions and the way to answer them. Further examples are available on the Web site www.self-assess.faststream.gov.uk. This and the next chapter are intended to provide additional practice questions. Further material is available in other Kogan Page publications.

The Fast Stream competition is fierce. Thousands of entrants compete for a few hundred places. In fact the Fast Stream often attracts over 10,000 applicants a year and only 20 per cent of these are successful. To succeed you will have to be very well prepared indeed. If you are serious about wanting to join the programme, set about a significant timetable of preparation. Be prepared to concentrate on the areas in which you do least well. To have any chance of success you will need to score consistently well across all the tests.

The test will be organized in the time-honoured fashion whereby you attend a test centre, with a room set out as an examination hall holding many small desks. There is a slight possibility that you may face a bank of computer terminals, depending on whether you do the computer administered version of the test.

Other candidates are very likely to be present. In some instances there may be a lot of other candidates. A test administrator will welcome you and explain the process. He or she will be following a prepared script, and will be happy to answer any questions, although the answers given may be rather brief or superficial. As previously mentioned, this is because the administrator is keen to ensure that all candidates (including those who have attended on other days and will not have heard your question) receive the same information and experience the same test conditions. So he or she will be reluctant to stray far from the script.

The Fast Stream is an intense competition and a major test of endurance. You will attempt a series or battery of tests, sat one after the other against straight time constraints over a number of hours. During the tests you really have to apply yourself if you are to show your true potential. When you leave the test centre you should feel worn out; otherwise don't expect to stand out from the crowd.

Page 1 of the Fast Stream information booklet describes the importance of recording your answers by fully blackening the appropriate answer box. Otherwise the mechanical marker will underscore or mis-score your paper. Note that some answers may require more than one answer box to be blackened fully. A separate piece of paper is provided for rough workings. Make no marks on your answer sheet other than your answers, as this risks the mechanical marking misinterpreting your answers.

Page 2 of the booklet provides some sound advice on test strategy. Pay particular attention to the advice on educated guessing, whereby if you do not know the answer to a question you eliminate as many incorrect answers as you can and then guess. Answering all questions pays in both the verbal and numerical test, but an analysis of the information provided on the test marking scheme shows that it includes penalties for incorrect answers. So resist radium guessing in these tests, but do still have a go at educated guessing.

Practice questions for the verbal test

You are allowed 28 minutes to complete the test block of this test. Further time is allowed for the introduction and practice block and experimental block. Each question comprises four sentences. The sentences are identified by the letters A–D, but the order in which they were originally written has been lost and the sentences are now in the wrong order. Your task is to put the sentences into the correct or original order.

You record your answer by placing the letters in the answer box in the order in which you think they were originally.

With practice many students see big improvements in their score for this type of exercise. For this reason I have provided lots of practice material. Allow yourself 50 seconds per question to complete the following practice examples.

The questions begin in a style where each sentence is separated, which many students report that they find more approachable than the actual test layout. The questions from 15 onwards switch to the style adopted in the real test, and you should do these as you get more accomplished.

1
A A professional homeopath, as a result of education, training and clinical experience, is competent to treat patients presenting with a wide variety of conditions.
B No one system can deal with all that an individual may need, or serve the entire population.
C Homeopathy may not always be the most appropriate form of treatment.

D Homeopathy is a unique system and therapeutic discipline that fulfils an important role in healthcare; it serves to prevent ill-health as well as being of benefit to most patients in both acute and chronic disease.

Answer: [   ]

2

A The walking season never ends; indeed each month brings its own character and invites you to repeat a walk at different times of the year.

B It is ideal for families, who do not need to join a club in order to do it.

C Walking and close contact with the real, living world are essential parts of growing up, especially in the age of the television.

D Walking is a natural activity that requires little in the way of money and gives enjoyment without a competitive element.

Answer: [   ]

3

A In those days shields were very large, and rose at the middle into two peaks with a hollow between them, so that Thafta, seen far off in the sea, with its two chief mountain peaks, and a cloven valley between them, looked exactly like a shield.

B Long ago in the small and mountainous island of Thafta lived a king named Umonico.

C The country was so rough that people kept no horses, but there were plenty of cattle.

D People used to say that Thafta 'lay like a shield upon the sea', which sounds as though it were a very flat country.

Answer: [   ]

4

A Once you've sat down somewhere inconvenient, do not spring up just because you've been asked politely.

B The quickest way to do this is to park on a double yellow line, which is the daily street protest undertaken by most city dwellers.

C To start this, you need to park yourself somewhere where the police will have to move you on.

D Civil disobedience is a legal requirement of any demonstration.

Answer:

5

A The range, manufactured by electronics giant Gizzmo, comprises an Internet-enabled washing machine, microwave oven and air conditioning unit, as well as the first 'smart fridge', which has an Internet connection and the capacity to form the hub of a future home network.

B The technology involved is already available to consumers.

C Home networking, as it's called, connects every appliance in the home, from your PC to your central heating, via a central hub, which can then be accessed and controlled via the Internet.

D Indeed, one company has already launched the first range of such appliances in the UK.

Answer:

6

A The Trojans gathered on a height in the plain, and Hector, shining in armour, went here and there, in front and rear, like a start that now gleams forth and now is hidden in a cloud.

B With dawn Agamemnon awoke, and fear had gone out of his heart.

C Then a great black cloud spread over the sky, and red was the rain that fell from it.

D He put on his armour, and arrayed the chiefs on foot in front of their chariots, and behind them came the spearmen, with the bowmen and slingers on the wings of the army.

Answer: [   ]

7

A At 3,560 ft, Snowdon is the highest mountain south of the Scottish Highlands.

B Its 845 square miles make only a slightly smaller area than the 866 square miles of the English Lake District.

C Snowdonia is the second largest national park in Great Britain.

D Over 500,000 people climb it each year.

Answer: [   ]

8

A They may seem like an arcane field of investigation: after all, are there not more pressing problems with extant species?

B But the development of a species, its transformations and final extinction, are all elements that can be applied to current-day biology.

C Their closest living relative is the horseshoe crab.

D Trilobites roamed the world's oceans some 500 million years ago.

Answer: [   ]

9

A The huge amount of energy is radiated out from the core and some eventually reaches Earth, keeping us alive.

B It has been doing this for 4,500 million years, but is still only halfway through its lifetime.

C The Sun is using up its mass at the rate of 4 million tonnes each second!

D It is a middle-aged star.

Answer:

10

A The same applies to spacecraft which operate in places where there is no atmosphere at all.

B Jet airliners fly at heights of 10,000 metres or more.

C Such aircraft are said to be pressurized.

D At such heights the atmosphere is so thin that the aircraft must have its own air supply with oxygen at the normal pressure.

Answer:

11

A This is usually caused by a reaction to pollen, and is therefore particularly common when flowers are open.

B The eyes may be affected in the same way, becoming itchy, sore and weepy.

C Many people suffer from hay fever.

D The lining of the nasal cavity becomes sensitive and inflamed and produces a large amount of mucous, so the nose runs and the person sneezes a lot.

Answer:

12

A   Particular finger positions or gestures of the hand, common to their age and civilization, delivered a message that was instantly recognized by those who understood the symbolism.

B   Since ancient times hands have been used in cave paintings, drawings, sculpture and fine art as symbols of communication.

C   European religious painting represented the Holy Trinity by the extended thumb, index, and middle fingers of a hand.

D   Ancient Egyptian and Semitic art, for example, depicted celestial power by a hand painted in the sky.

Answer: [   ]

13

A   Without food, small birds can quickly starve to death.

B   Somehow they must maintain reserves at a level that allows them to avoid both starvation and predation.

C   Too little fat and they may starve to death, while too much increases the energy required for flight, causing them to be slower, less agile and more at risk of predation.

D   To survive a long, cold night or periods during the day without eating, birds need to put on fat reserves.

Answer: [   ]

14

A   The sapwood is less dense and therefore softer than the heartwood.

B   The heartwood is extremely dense and hard and its only job is to support the tree.

C   It is therefore much wetter than the heartwood.

D   It provides support too, but it also carries water and mineral salts (sap) up the trunk.

Answer: [   ]

15

A A series of islands or chains in the head or heart lines may point to an imbalance of the biochemistry due to mineral deficiencies. **B** It follows that any impairment of the lines reveals that the constitution is somehow weakened. **C** Clear, strong lines in the hand are thought to reflect robust health. **D** A similar effect on the life line reveals poor vitality and a weakened constitution.

Answer:

16

A Its plan to increase the amount of municipal waste we recycle to 33 per cent by 2015 has been described as 'depressingly unambitious' by a parliamentary committee, as most Western nations have already surpassed this level. **B** In parts of Belgium, for example, 72 per cent of biodegradable waste is recycled or composted, compared with about 11 per cent in the UK. **C** The government has been criticized for its laissez-faire attitude. **D** While other countries are well on their way to meeting the EU levels by recycling and composting, the UK is lagging far behind.

Answer:

17

A The attacks are often brought on by pollen or dust, or occasionally by some kind of food to which the person is allergic. **B** This makes it difficult to breathe and the person wheezes. **C** Asthma is serious. **D** The muscles in the walls of the bronchioles contract, so the tubes get narrower.

Answer:

18

A   A 20-year study has found that taking 300–400 micrograms a day of this B-vitamin can cut your risk by 20 per cent.   **B** Folic acid, long recommended to women trying to conceive, could prevent strokes too.   **C**   It helps break down homocysteine, an amino acid that occurs naturally in the body and has been linked to artery-wall damage.   **D**   Folic acid is found in broccoli, tomatoes, kidney beans, liver, some citrus fruits and leafy green vegetables such as spinach, or is available in pill form.

Answer:

19

A   If enlargement of the EU goes ahead, it will increase by 10 member states by the beginning of 2004.   **B**   When these countries attain membership, hundreds of thousands will want to move to the west in search of higher incomes, and in time, as citizens of the EU, they will be perfectly entitled to do so.   **C** Arguably the most important fact about immigration is that in the next two decades much of it will be lawful.   **D**   Much of the small print remains to be agreed, but it is likely that the EU will increase by 30 per cent.

Answer:

20

A   Under the plan the group would sell its private equity division to its management who would then manage the 2 billion of investments owned by the group.   **B**   The decision has forced the group to consider selling its own private equity operation in order to avoid a conflict of interest.   **C**   The move would see Axis surrender control of its equity investments in favour of funds managed externally.   **D**   Axis is preparing to invest 650 million US dollars in Ava Investors, the Orlando based private equity firm set up to manage the wealth of the billionaire Savini family.

Answer:

21

A　Latuga's banks have lent £100 million at an annual negative interest rate of 1 per cent.　**B**　This means that instead of Latuga paying interest on the loan the banks will pay Latuga £1 million a year interest.　**C**　Latuga, the world's biggest producer of tinned greens, turned the banking world on its head by taking out the first ever negative interest loan.　**D**　The banks were happy to agree the loan because it has allowed them to acquire bonds and shares which are forecast to grow by as much as 5 per cent a year.

Answer: _____

22

A　The arts in the UK must to an observer seem to be booming, with new galleries opening in the capital to great acclaim, thriving regional institutions, and ambitious plans to open a major centre of contemporary art in the North West.　**B**　Add to this the fact that three years ago the Chancellor gave the arts a considerable financial boost and the National Lottery Fund has provided millions of pounds of lottery money to provide new or renovate existing venues.　**C**　Yet the Arts Council expresses fears that even after such record spending, some arts institutions are struggling to survive and risk financial collapse. **D**　There is some evidence to support this surprising view if one compares the funding for museums and galleries per capita across Europe, for then one realizes that the UK continues to lag behind its neighbours in arts expenditure.

Answer: _____

23

A　But if the government does about the nation's diet and level of exercise what it has done about most health risks such as smoking and drinking alcohol, which is very little or nothing, then the level of obesity will continue to rise and the health of the nation will continue to fall.   **B**   In the face of such likely government inaction, the only real alternative engines for change are education and litigation, but unlike smoking and drinking there is nothing intrinsically unhealthy about eating, so it is hard to imagine how recourse to the courts could force change on the nation's eating habits.   **C**   That leaves education, and given that fast-food chains and sugar drink companies have a massive presence in almost every campus, state school and even hospital, it is hard to imagine how the cash-starved educational institutions can alone counter the junk food movement.   **D**   If the government is willing to regulate to force disclosure of the content of what we eat, get junk food out of schools, make available more healthy alternatives, and install bike racks in public places to encourage more exercise, then the health of the nation will improve.

Answer: [   ]

24

A   Some economists have been expressing fears for a considerable length of time about an unsustainable boom which could turn into a bust.   **B**   The admission comes in a report to the Home Affairs Committee setting out the implications of the continued rise, fuelled by low unemployment, low interest rates and a shortage of housing stock.   **C**   In a startling reversal the government has acknowledged that house price inflation is a significant problem rather than just an issue.   **D**   The report identified that the issue became a problem for first-time buyers in London and the South East, and for professionals who could not afford to live in this region, so creating shortages of essential workers in hospitals, schools and the Civil Service.

Answer: [   ]

25
A   This time a synchronized recession took place whereby all the major economies slowed down and took with them many others, including Argentina, Mexico, Singapore and Taiwan. **B**   The IT and telecommunications driven fall in investment expenditure began in the United States and spread to the world's other economies, leading to worldwide economic recession.   **C**   The bursting of the hi-tech bubble is the most important reason for the slowing growth, but it has been made worse by the fact that each of the major economies has its own home grown problems which exacerbated the downturn.   **D** In the two previous economic downturns, one or more of the biggest economies has been able to avoid recession.

Answer: [   ]

26
A   Fay travelled to the same designation by train third class with her battered suitcase and few possessions; she hoped to find work teaching English but when the war intervened she volunteered to work in a Red Cross hospital.   **B**   The two women were to meet in the great city under the most unlikely circumstances.   **C**   Her family had fallen out of the middle class into poverty, and her marriage to a second-rate musician had ended sterile and pointless, but she look forward to a new life with courage and enthusiasm.   **D**   Lorenza went to Roma in a chauffeur-driven limousine; she was the daughter of a Venetian aristocrat whose family boasted two Doges from the 17th century, and her life to that point had been typical of her class, with high society parties and travel.

Answer: [   ]

27
A   First, our economy is driven by expenditure on luxury goods, and because they are luxury they are non-essential and so can be avoided altogether if the price becomes too great or

the spare cash we have in our pocket each month becomes too little.   **B**   Second, the potential housing bubble and the difficulty being experienced by public sector workers struggling to afford a home is peculiar to the South East, so why apply a general interest rate increase in an effort to address a regional problem?   **C**   I would argue that interest rates should be left unchanged and nothing done to the rate in order to tackle a housing problem that is not creating general inflationary pressure.   **D**   The property boom and the profits people are making from it may be the only thing preventing our economy sliding into recession, so why risk it?

Answer: [   ]

28

A   Hard on her heels is the US Deputy Secretary of State, who is expected to emphasize the fact that they also expect a crack down on its most polluting industries as a matter of urgency in order to ensure that the entry conditions to the treaty are realized.   **B**   In the diplomatic game of grandmother's footsteps, in which the world powers try to coax China to sign the environmental treaty, they seem to have forced the Beijing authorities to realize that they must take the first half step.   **C** If the authorities fail to control the level of omissions they are vulnerable to the unfair charge that corruption is preventing action; this, on top of the threatened diplomatic and economic isolation, is thought to be sufficient to ensure China will become both a signatory and a compliant member within the next three years.   **D**   Today the President of the European Union will deliver to the Chinese authorities the uncompromising message, endorsed by the Union Member States, that failure to follow words with actions could lead to diplomatic isolation.

Answer: [   ]

29

A   The areas of the country identified with the worst problems were mainly located in the South East of the country, along with North Yorkshire and the Lake District.   **B**   It comes on the day a senior minister called for 100,000 new homes a year to be built in villages and hamlets to create and sustain populations large enough to support rural shops and schools.   **C**   The need for more and better homes was reported to be most acute in the social housing sector, yet that sector was dwindling as tenants exercised the right to buy in areas of high demand where thousands of people on low incomes or living on benefits are priced out of the property market.   **D**   The need for more social housing is outlined in a stark report from the Countryside Agency, the government's main advisor on rural issues, which was published today.

Answer:

30

A   The commission also wants insurers to be legally bound to provide compulsory cover for pedestrians and cyclists involved in accidents with cars.   **B**   A shake up of the law governing the industry across Europe will make it far easier for individuals to switch insurance companies.   **C**   Plans were announced by the European Commission that should lead to greater competition in the vehicle insurance market.   **D**   It should mean that companies are no longer able to restrict the length of time motorists may keep their vehicles in EU states other than the ones in which they are registered.

Answer:

31

A The commission is drawing up a dossier of information to demonstrate to the Home Office that women are being unfairly excluded from the force and that the test has very little bearing on the work of the police. **B** The commission argues that a police officer very rarely has to run down the street after a criminal, and so whether or not they can run fast or have a firm grip is irrelevant to the job and prevents many able women applicants from becoming officers. **C** The present test involves an endurance run, and upper body and hand strength tests which the commission would like to see replaced with a health screening. **D** The Equality Commission is pressing the Home Office to change the fitness test used for the recruitment of police officers, which it is argued is unfairly biased towards male applicants.

Answer:

32

A The study found that 70 per cent of children reported that their dreams reflected their viewing habits, while only 60 per cent of adults reported that television influenced their dreams. **B** Research has found that children's dreams are influenced more by television than adults', while adults' dreams are affected most by what they are reading. **C** Fantasy books were linked to a higher rate of nightmares amongst both children and adults, with children, for example, reporting that scary books caused nightmares. **D** The analysis found apparent links between respondents' dreams and the subject of their reading.

Answer:

33
A Sunday's vote is expected to be noticeable in one other respect, as the socialist vote stood firm while generally the left vote collapsed. **B** Sunday's vote places in perspective some of the more excitable commentary in America on France becoming a fascist state. **C** On Sunday when the second round of the French parliamentary elections is completed it is likely that the country will have a president and parliament of the same political persuasion for the first time for a number of years. **D** The far right vote also collapsed because of the centre right tougher policies on crime and immigration, and because of the poor standard of the right wing candidates, many of whom hardly bothered to campaign.

Answer:

Practice questions for the quantitative reasoning test

Section 1 of the numerical test comprises a test block of questions, which you are allowed 10 minutes to complete. The test booklet provides the following description of the question type. Each question consists of five rows of three or four figures. The numerical relationship is the same between each row. You have to identify the numerical relationship in the first row and use it to work out what the missing number is in the fifth row.

Try the following examples. They get harder as you progress. Full explanations are provided with the answers. Many students have found that practice can make a big difference in performance in this type of question, so again lots of practice material is provided. Realistic question formats and answer boxes are used.

1

A	B	C
9	4	22
4	2	10
11	7	29
18	2	38
3	?	19

0	0	0
1	1	1
2	2	2
3	3	3
4	4	4
5	5	5
6	6	6
7	7	7
8	8	8
9	9	9

2

A	B	C
4	17	25
12	2	26
3	3	9
14	4	32
17	1	?

0	0	0
1	1	1
2	2	2
3	3	3
4	4	4
5	5	5
6	6	6
7	7	7
8	8	8
9	9	9

3

A	B	C
5	2	12
3	12	18
5	4	14
7	5	19
?	7	19

0	0	0
1	1	1
2	2	2
3	3	3
4	4	4
5	5	5
6	6	6
7	7	7
8	8	8
9	9	9

4

A	B	C
4	1	7
8	4	20
2	3	11
4	3	13
11	32	?

0	0	0
1	1	1
2	2	2
3	3	3
4	4	4
5	5	5
6	6	6
7	7	7
8	8	8
9	9	9

5

A	B	C
4	15	49
12	9	39
175	19	232
25	14	67
3	?	18

0	0	0
1	1	1
2	2	2
3	3	3
4	4	4
5	5	5
6	6	6
7	7	7
8	8	8
9	9	9

6

A	B	C
17	2	23
12	3	21
15	5	30
14	2	20
?	3	28

0	0	0
1	1	1
2	2	2
3	3	3
4	4	4
5	5	5
6	6	6
7	7	7
8	8	8
9	9	9

7

A	B	C
4	3	4
3	6	−1
14	3	24
1	2	−1
12	6	?

0	0	0
1	1	1
2	2	2
3	3	3
4	4	4
5	5	5
6	6	6
7	7	7
8	8	8
9	9	9

8

A	B	C
12	1	22
34	13	54
3	0	5
15	12	17
21	14	?

0	0	0
1	1	1
2	2	2
3	3	3
4	4	4
5	5	5
6	6	6
7	7	7
8	8	8
9	9	9

9

A	B	C
14	13	14
21	2	39
3	2	3
2	1	2
5	9	?

0	0	0
1	1	1
2	2	2
3	3	3
4	4	4
5	5	5
6	6	6
7	7	7
8	8	8
9	9	9

10

A	B	C
7	26	–10
3	14	–10
2	6	0
5	20	–10
13	38	?

0	0	0
1	1	1
2	2	2
3	3	3
4	4	4
5	5	5
6	6	6
7	7	7
8	8	8
9	9	9

11

A	B	C
6	12	12
2	2	8
15	66	–42
68	344	–280
123	16	?

0	0	0
1	1	1
2	2	2
3	3	3
4	4	4
5	5	5
6	6	6
7	7	7
8	8	8
9	9	9

12

A	B	C
1	1	4
24	60	24
2	–5	22
6	8	20
11	25	?

0	0	0
1	1	1
2	2	2
3	3	3
4	4	4
5	5	5
6	6	6
7	7	7
8	8	8
9	9	9

13

A	B	C
35	60	85
25	65	90
10	10	160
24	48	108
50	22	?

0	0	0
1	1	1
2	2	2
3	3	3
4	4	4
5	5	5
6	6	6
7	7	7
8	8	8
9	9	9

14

A	B	C
37	27	116
88	0	92
120	19	41
25	92	63
?	0	172

0	0	0
1	1	1
2	2	2
3	3	3
4	4	4
5	5	5
6	6	6
7	7	7
8	8	8
9	9	9

15

A	B	C
17	77	86
12	32	136
15	80	85
14	14	152
25	?	83

0	0	0
1	1	1
2	2	2
3	3	3
4	4	4
5	5	5
6	6	6
7	7	7
8	8	8
9	9	9

16

A	B	C
822	144	678
728	214	514
373	212	161
882	215	667
877	678	?

0	0	0
1	1	1
2	2	2
3	3	3
4	4	4
5	5	5
6	6	6
7	7	7
8	8	8
9	9	9

17

A	B	C
8.4	7.2	1.2
17.8	14.7	3.1
27.3	13.2	14.1
92.4	77.1	15.3
78.3	43.2	?

0	0	0
1	1	1
2	2	2
3	3	3
4	4	4
5	5	5
6	6	6
7	7	7
8	8	8
9	9	9

Note: in these questions the columns correspond to 10s, 1s and 0.1s

18

A	B	C
71	12	59
82	11	71
93	10	83
104	9	95
115	8	?

0	0	0
1	1	1
2	2	2
3	3	3
4	4	4
5	5	5
6	6	6
7	7	7
8	8	8
9	9	9

19

A	B	C
3.3	0	10.89
7.3	0	53.29
13	0	169
19	0	361
20	0	?

0	0	0
1	1	1
2	2	2
3	3	3
4	4	4
5	5	5
6	6	6
7	7	7
8	8	8
9	9	9

20

A	B	C
3	12	9
4	32	16
5	14	25
6	12	36
7	8	?

0	0	0
1	1	1
2	2	2
3	3	3
4	4	4
5	5	5
6	6	6
7	7	7
8	8	8
9	9	9

21

A	B	C
5	400	25
10	395	100
15	390	225
20	385	400
25	380	?

0	0	0
1	1	1
2	2	2
3	3	3
4	4	4
5	5	5
6	6	6
7	7	7
8	8	8
9	9	9

22

A	B	C
4	1	11
16	44	4
72	25	191
26	26	52
50	25	?

0	0	0
1	1	1
2	2	2
3	3	3
4	4	4
5	5	5
6	6	6
7	7	7
8	8	8
9	9	9

23

A	B	C
14	15	27
12	9	27
5	5	10
4	5	7
3	5	?

0	0	0
1	1	1
2	2	2
3	3	3
4	4	4
5	5	5
6	6	6
7	7	7
8	8	8
9	9	9

24

A	B	C
17	2	49
12	3	33
15	5	40
14	2	40
13	13	?

0	0	0
1	1	1
2	2	2
3	3	3
4	4	4
5	5	5
6	6	6
7	7	7
8	8	8
9	9	9

25

A	B	C
5	3	14
17	3	50
2	3	5
4	3	11
11	3	?

0	0	0
1	1	1
2	2	2
3	3	3
4	4	4
5	5	5
6	6	6
7	7	7
8	8	8
9	9	9

Harder questions

1

A	B	C
9	4	5
625	400	45
1600	900	70
100	4	12
225	25	?

0	0	0
1	1	1
2	2	2
3	3	3
4	4	4
5	5	5
6	6	6
7	7	7
8	8	8
9	9	9

2

A	B	C
49	4	9
64	9	11
81	16	13
100	36	16
144	64	?

0	0	0
1	1	1
2	2	2
3	3	3
4	4	4
5	5	5
6	6	6
7	7	7
8	8	8
9	9	9

3

A	B	C
576	4	26
529	16	27
484	64	30
441	121	32
400	100	?

0	0	0
1	1	1
2	2	2
3	3	3
4	4	4
5	5	5
6	6	6
7	7	7
8	8	8
9	9	9

4

A	B	C
12	4	36
18	4	30
14	5	61
29	6	79
15	5	?

0	0	0
1	1	1
2	2	2
3	3	3
4	4	4
5	5	5
6	6	6
7	7	7
8	8	8
9	9	9

5

A	B	C
100	9	143
200	14	388
300	12	132
400	15	275
200	12	?

0	0	0
1	1	1
2	2	2
3	3	3
4	4	4
5	5	5
6	6	6
7	7	7
8	8	8
9	9	9

6

A	B	C
200	20	1000
150	22	1302
12	4	36
488	14	100
250	20	?

0	0	0
1	1	1
2	2	2
3	3	3
4	4	4
5	5	5
6	6	6
7	7	7
8	8	8
9	9	9

7

A	B	C
2	3	24
5	12	240
13	3	156
6	10	240
12	2	?

0	0	0
1	1	1
2	2	2
3	3	3
4	4	4
5	5	5
6	6	6
7	7	7
8	8	8
9	9	9

8

A	B	C
4	6	96
4	7	112
4	5	80
4	4	64
4	8	?

0	0	0
1	1	1
2	2	2
3	3	3
4	4	4
5	5	5
6	6	6
7	7	7
8	8	8
9	9	9

9

A	B	C
12	5	240
5	4	80
6	8	192
5	12	240
10	5	?

0	0	0
1	1	1
2	2	2
3	3	3
4	4	4
5	5	5
6	6	6
7	7	7
8	8	8
9	9	9

10

A	B	C
16	64	4
144	225	3
1	16	3
4	16	2
16	256	?

0	0	0
1	1	1
2	2	2
3	3	3
4	4	4
5	5	5
6	6	6
7	7	7
8	8	8
9	9	9

11

A	B	C
256	1024	16
25	900	25
16	256	12
64	256	8
1600	2500	?

0	0	0
1	1	1
2	2	2
3	3	3
4	4	4
5	5	5
6	6	6
7	7	7
8	8	8
9	9	9

12

A	B	C
1225	2025	10
625	2025	20
625	625	0
49	2025	38
9	169	?

0	0	0
1	1	1
2	2	2
3	3	3
4	4	4
5	5	5
6	6	6
7	7	7
8	8	8
9	9	9

13

A	B	C
124	42	194
80	45	235
22	148	190
35	170	155
50	145	?

0	0	0
1	1	1
2	2	2
3	3	3
4	4	4
5	5	5
6	6	6
7	7	7
8	8	8
9	9	9

14

A	B	C
200	67	93
45	98	217
76	22	262
40	195	125
104	256	?

0	0	0
1	1	1
2	2	2
3	3	3
4	4	4
5	5	5
6	6	6
7	7	7
8	8	8
9	9	9

15

A	B	C
10	20	330
40	30	290
70	40	250
150	50	160
220	60	?

0	0	0
1	1	1
2	2	2
3	3	3
4	4	4
5	5	5
6	6	6
7	7	7
8	8	8
9	9	9

16

A	B	C
4	4	12
10	5	45
1	5	0
5	1	4
5	10	?

0	0	0
1	1	1
2	2	2
3	3	3
4	4	4
5	5	5
6	6	6
7	7	7
8	8	8
9	9	9

Practice questions for the data interpretation test

This block comprises section 2 of the numerical test. In the real test you have 28 minutes to complete the data interpretation test block of questions. Extra time is spent on the introduction and on practice questions and an experimental block.

The test comprises tables of data or passages of information, each of which has three associated questions. Five alternative answers are given, from which you must select the right answer.

It sometimes helps to look to the suggested answers before you attempt lengthy calculations, as you can possibly rule out some of the suggested answers and then estimate the correct answer by rounding sums up or down to more convenient figures. Try the following practice questions.

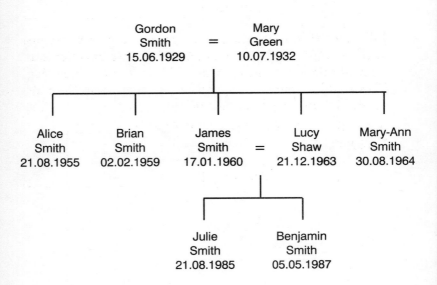

Figure 4.1   The Smith family tree

1. How old will Brian be on 01.02.2004?

    A 44   B 45   C 46   D 47   E 48   F 49

    Answer: [   ]

2. What is the age difference between Alice and Julie?

    A 21 years   B 25 years   C 26 years   D 30 years
    E 32 years   F 34 years

    Answer: [   ]

3. Gordon died in an accident before Mary-Ann was born.
    Alice was only eight, Brian and James were both four.
    When did he die?

    A August 1963   B October 1963   C November 1963
    D January 1964   E May 1964   F June 1964

    Answer: [   ]

4. Julie and Alice share the same birthday. For presents one
    year Alice gives Julie a cheque and Julie presents her aunt
    with a bouquet of roses worth £15.00. Julie quickly calcu-
    lates that her aunt has spent 25 per cent more than she
    received. How much money did Julie gain?

    A £2.50   B £5.00   C £10.00   D £15.00   E £17.50
    F £20.00

    Answer: [   ]

Table 4.1 2001 top 20 earners (taken as an average across the whole of each profession)

Rank	Occupation	Salary 2001 (£)	Salary 1991 (£)
1	General managers (large companies)	110,341	52,449
2	Barristers	78,549	30,813
3	Senior general administrators, Civil Service	61,993	39,944
4	Treasurers & company financial managers	59,121	25,692
5	Aircraft pilots	57,328	42,055
6	Managers in mining & energy industries	48,916	32,017
7	Doctors	48,235	30,822
8	Insurance underwriters, claims assessors	46,034	28,928
9	Management consultants	45,313	29,914
10	Judges and court officers	45,022	28,435
11	IT managers	43,268	27,440
12	Work study managers	42,867	26,099
13	Police officers (Inspector and above)	41,984	30,660
14	Chemical engineers	40,926	26,657
15	Air, commodity & ship brokers	40,421	33,144
16	Solicitors	39,775	28,081
17	Marketing & sales managers	39,750	25,692
18	Personnel managers	37,216	25,187
19	Physicists, geologists & meteorologists	36,829	25,890
20	Air traffic planners & controllers	36,797	27,476

5. Which occupation showed the lowest percentage change between 1991 and 2001?

A Senior general administrators: Civil Service
B Aircraft pilots
C Doctors
D Police officers (Inspector and above)
E Air, commodity & ship brokers
F Air traffic planners & controllers

Answer:

6.   What is the difference in average earnings between 1991 and 2001?

A £14,961.50   B £15,649.10   C £16,591.40   D £16,914.50   E £19,164.50   F £19,654.10

Answer: [   ]

7.   By what minimum percentage must air traffic planners & controllers increase their 1991 wage to become top of the list in 2001?

A 151.1   B 199.9   C 252.4   D 301.6   E 355.3   F 410.8

Answer: [   ]

8.   Professional athletes earned £17,652 in 1991. If their earnings were to increase by 166.3 per cent where would they rank in 2001?

Answer: [   ]

Table 4.2   Gross weekly earnings of full-time adult employees in Great Britain

| | | Median gross weekly earnings (£) | | |
	Manual men	Non-manual men	Manual women	Non-manual women
1986	163.4	219.4	101.1	131.5
1987	173.9	235.7	108.2	142.2
1988	188.0	259.7	115.6	157.1
1989	203.9	285.7	125.9	173.5
1990	221.3	312.1	137.3	191.8
1991	235.4	332.2	147.4	211.1
1992	250.7	353.4	156.6	227.6

9. Which year saw the greatest increase in earnings for manual women?

    A 1986–7   B 1987–8   C 1988–9   D 1989–90   E 1990–1
    F 1991–2

    Answer:

10. How much more must non-manual women earn to bring them in line with men in similar occupations in 1992?

    A £23.10   B £71.00   C £94.10   D £102.70   E £125.80
    F £196.80

    Answer:

11. By what percentage have non-manual men's earnings increased between 1988 and 1992?

    A 36.1%   B 42.5%   C 45.6%   D 49.7%   E 54.8%
    F 61.1%

    Answer:

12. What was the average weekly wage difference between manual and non-manual men between 1986 and 1992?

    A £79.80   B £80.23   C £81.40   D £81.90   E £82.20
    F £83.60

    Answer:

13. If the fees had not been transferred to the Polytechnics and Colleges Funding Council in April 1989, how much would Higher, Further and Adult Education have received in 1991?

    A £993 million   B £3,734 million   C £4,727 million
    D £6,401 million   E £10,135 million   F £11,128 million

    Answer:

Table 4.3   Government expenditure on education in real terms: by type

UK	£ million		
	1970–71	1980–81	1991–92
Schools			
Nursery	58	114	
Primary	4,713	5,886	
Secondary	5,523	7,754	8,287
Special	442	917	1,280
Higher, Further and Adult Education*	2,884	3,517	3,734
Polytechnics and Colleges Funding Council	—	—	993
Universities	2,325	2,698	2,668
Other education expenditure	706	1,027	1,394
Total	**16,651**	**21,913**	**25,976**
Related education expenditure	2,727	2,678	2,995
VAT on above expenditure	2,132	2,705	5,070
Total expenditure	**21,510**	**27,296**	**34,041**
Total expenditure as a percentage of GDP	**5.2**	**5.5**	**5.1**

* Includes fees for polytechnics and colleges transferred to the Polytechnics and Colleges Funding Council in April 1989

14. What is the percentage increase in expenditure on secondary education between 1970 and 1991?

    A 6.9%   B 40.4%   C 24.6%   D 31.3%   E 45.5%
    F 50.0%

    Answer: [   ]

15. What was the total GDP for 1991?

    A £34,041 million   B £58,725 million
    C £509,333 million   D £568,059 million
    E £667,471 million   F £680,820 million

    Answer: [   ]

16.   What was the rate of VAT in 1980?
A 7.5%   B 11.0%   C 12.5%   D 14.0%   E 15.0%
F 17.5%

Answer: [   ]

Practice questions for the analysis of information test

There are two types of question in this test block. They are called type A and B. You have 47 minutes to complete the test block. Once again there is extra time allowed for the completion of an introduction and practice block and an experimental block.

Type A questions comprise a passage and a group of three statements that relate to the passage. Your task is to decide from the information in the passage whether each statement is true, false or it is impossible to tell. It is important that you take the contents of the passage at face value. Do not be tempted to bring you own views or knowledge into your deliberations.

Type B questions comprise a passage of information, a question and a list of information. You have to decide which of the items of information you need to order to answer the question.

Practise on the following examples.

Type A questions

Passage 1

An underground railway system is made up of five lines of equal length, all of which run in completely straight lines. The blue line runs north/south and intersects with the red line that runs east/west. The green line runs from southeast to northwest and intersects the red line east of the blue line. The yellow line runs from north-east and intersects the blue line north of the red line. The grey line runs parallel to the green line, and intersects the blue line south of the red line.

1. The angle between the red and blue line at their point of intersection is 90 degrees.

    True   False   Impossible to say

    Answer: [   ]

2. If the grey line were to intersect the red line it would do so west of the green line.

    True   False   Impossible to say

    Answer: [   ]

3. The green line intersects the blue line east of the intersection between the yellow line and the blue line.

    True   False   Impossible to say

    Answer: [   ]

4. The easternmost point of the green line is farther east than the easternmost point of the red line.

    True   False   Impossible to say

    Answer: [   ]

Passage 2

The financial markets are seeking high yields and safe havens, which should boost the Australian and New Zealand dollar, but the Asian currencies have firmed versus the dollar too. Economic growth in East Asia appears to be on a sound footing but the Yen's recent strengthening is not regarded as sustainable. Interest rates in the eurozone and UK are unlikely to move for the next few months. These rates are likely to remain unchanged for as much as a year, and then any rise is likely to be small.

5.   A rate decrease is expected in the eurozone shortly.

   True   False   Impossible to say

   Answer: [   ]

6.   The Yen is expected to weaken.

   True   False   Impossible to say

   Answer: [   ]

7.   New Zealand's currency will remain aligned with the Australian currency.

   True   False   Impossible to say

   Answer: [   ]

Passage 3

In a league of teams, a win scores two points, and a draw scores one point. Team 1 has four more points than Team 2, which has seven fewer points than Team 3. Team 4 has won more games than Team 1 and has lost no games. Team 5, on 17 points, is five points ahead of Team 4. Team 6 has four more points than Team 2. All teams have played the same number of games.

8.   Team 4 has more points than Team 1.

   True   False   Impossible to say

   Answer: [   ]

9.   Team 6 has more points than Team 3.

   True   False   Impossible to say

   Answer: [   ]

10. Team 2 is bottom of the league.

    True   False   Impossible to say

    Answer: [   ]

Passage 4

The terms 'psychometric tests' and 'psychological testing' are used interchangeably to describe tools which are essentially sophisticated devices designed to measure individual differences in a number of areas such as intelligence and ability. If used appropriately, tests can enhance decision making and enable managers to develop more informed and accurate forecasts of an individual's potential. To achieve this it is essential that the test is integrated into the decision-making process. Even the best tests available are only as good as the process of which they form a part, and flawed decisions can still be made.

11. A psychometric test is the single best predictor of likely job performance.

    True   False   Impossible to say

    Answer: [   ]

12. Psychological tests are most effective as tools to predict individual performance when integrated into the decision-making process.

    True   False   Impossible to say

    Answer: [   ]

13. The principal point of the passage can be summed up as the assertion that the ability to measure individual differences allows a manager to forecast an individual's potential.

    True   False   Impossible to say

    Answer: [   ]

Passage 5

During a 14-day holiday which starts on a Sunday, there are three days where the sky is clear all day. Of the 11 days that there is some cloud, it rains on four different days. On one occasion it rains on consecutive days. On two occasions the sky is clear all day after it has rained on the day before. It rains on both of the Saturdays, one Friday and one Wednesday.

14.   The days of the week on which it rains consecutively are a Friday and a Saturday.

   True   False   Impossible to say

   Answer: [   ]

15.   The sky is clear on at least one Sunday.

   True   False   Impossible to say

   Answer: [   ]

16.   The highest number of consecutive days without rain is six days.

   True   False   Impossible to say

   Answer: [   ]

Passage 6

A stakeholder pension plan is a simple and tax-efficient way of saving specifically for your retirement. All contributions qualify for tax relief at the highest rate you pay, and growth is free of UK income tax and capital gains tax (the tax on dividends from UK companies cannot be reclaimed). With a few exceptions anyone can pay up to £3,600 gross a year regardless of their age or employment status. Over this level further amounts can be invested based on your earnings in the current tax year or any of the previous five tax years and your age. So, for example, those aged between 46 and 50 years of age can invest up to 25 per cent of their earnings, while those aged up to 35 can invest 17.5 per cent. In general the older the worker, the greater a percentage he or she is allowed to invest. Savers can increase or reduce their contributions at any time, or make one-off payments within the overall limits determined by their age and earnings.

17. You will be able to invest more than £3600 a year into your stakeholder plan if you meet the age requirement.

    True   False   Impossible to say

    Answer: [ ]

18. Someone 27 years of age can invest £5,250 a year of his/her salary of £30,000.

    True   False   Impossible to say

    Answer: [ ]

19. If you pay tax at the higher rate of 40 per cent then your contributions will qualify for 40 per cent tax relief.

    True   False   Impossible to say

    Answer: [ ]

Passage 7

For sale is an exceptional property overlooking the marketplace with a triple aspect reception room commanding views across the popular area. The property is accessed via its own entrance on the ground floor and is arranged over the first, second and third floors of a period property. It comprises approximately 2,000 sq feet of living space. On the second floor are both the bedrooms, of which the master bedroom measures some 18 feet in length. On the third floor is a spectacular open plan kitchen/family room with a raised dining area and wrought iron spiral staircase affording access to a roof terrace. Underground parking is available by separate agreement.

20. All the bedrooms are on the floor below the kitchen.

    True   False   Impossible to say

    Answer: [   ]

21. The reception room is 18 feet in length with commanding views of the marketplace.

    True   False   Impossible to say

    Answer: [   ]

22. The reception room is on the first floor.

    True   False   Impossible to say

    Answer: [   ]

Passage 8

The term 'operating environment' refers to the interaction of an information system (typically a computer) with its user. The means of communication between the system, its hardware and software, and the user is called the user interface. The term 'software' can be used to describe both systems software and applications software. The first of these controls the computer's operating systems; the second relates to the user-related programs. The user interface is also called the human computer interface. Ideally it should be as easy to use as possible, so that the users do not have to study instruction manuals. The interface consists of, for example, cursors, prompts, icons and menus. Prompts can be either visual or audible. Interfaces can be either command driven, menu driven or graphical. Command driven interfaces are fast to use once you have learnt the commands which are inputted through a keyboard. Menu driven interfaces are much more user friendly, and can be inputted with either a mouse or keyboard.

23. A keyboard is an example of a command interface.
     True   False   Impossible to say

                        Answer: [   ]

24. Applications software is user related.
     True   False   Impossible to say

                        Answer: [   ]

25. The human computer interface is a means of communi-
     cation between the system, its hardware, software and the
     user.
     True   False   Impossible to say

                        Answer: [   ]

Passage 9

Kinematics is the branch of mathematics that deals with the motion of a particle in terms of displacement, velocity and acceleration, without considering the forces that may be required to cause the motion. For motion in a straight line, the distinction between distance and displacement is only that displacement may be positive or negative to indicate direction, whereas distance is always taken as positive. The same point can be made about speed and velocity. Velocity in a straight line may be positive or negative, depending on the direction, whereas speed is always positive. Kinematics can be contrasted with the subject of dynamics, which is concerned with the motion of a particle in response to forces that act on it.

26. Negative values can be used to indicate direction for both velocity and displacement.

    True   False   Impossible to say

    Answer: [   ]

27. In dynamics speed is always attributed a positive value.

    True   False   Impossible to say

    Answer: [   ]

28. Kinematics is concerned with the motion of a particle in a straight line but does not concern itself with the forces that act on the particle.

    True   False   Impossible to say

    Answer: [   ]

Passage 10

A depression is an area of low barometric pressure, which is usually responsible for periods of unsettled weather and often accompanied with strong winds. Depressions occur most frequently in middle and high latitudes. (The most severe storms occur in the low latitudes but these tropical revolving storms must be classified differently from a depression because of the sheer violence they unleash.) Depressions in the northern hemisphere generate winds in an anticlockwise direction, while in the southern hemisphere the winds generated blow in the opposite direction. Most depressions move at speeds up to 40 miles per hour. They last about three to five days and gradually slow down as the low barometric pressure fills. The wind strengths are reported on synoptic charts by the closeness of the isobar lines; the closer the lines, the stronger the wind strengths. The approach of a depression can be forecast by a fall in barometric pressure and by cloud formations.

29. In Australia depressions generate winds in a clockwise direction.

    True   False   Impossible to say

    Answer: [   ]

30. If a depression passes directly over a town, the wind direction shifts through a total of 180 degrees.

    True   False   Impossible to say

    Answer: [   ]

31. If you point your face directly into the wind of a depression in the northern hemisphere, your right ear will point towards the centre of the depression.

    True   False   Impossible to say

    Answer: [   ]

Passage 11

Both sides of a high street are made up of two identical rows of 20 uninterrupted shops exactly opposite each other. There is only one example of each type of shop. Between the pharmacist and the newsagent there are two other shops. Directly across the road from the newsagent is an off-licence. The optician is next door to the insurance broker and two shops away from the off-licence. The pedestrian crossing outside the pharmacist crosses over to the post office, with a clothes shop on one side and butcher on the other. The bus stop is directly across the road from the optician.

32. The pharmacist is on the same side of the road as the insurance broker.

    True   False   Impossible to say

    Answer: [   ]

33. The bus stop is on the same side of the road as the pharmacist.

   True   False   Impossible to say

   Answer: [   ]

34. The optician is next door to the butcher.

   True   False   Impossible to say

   Answer: [   ]

Passage 12

Begin laying the wooden laminate floor in a left-hand corner, with wedges between the boards and the wall, and with the tongues facing into the room. Start the second row with the piece left over from the first row. Leave at least 50 cm between end joints. Apply glue along the whole of the upper side of the groove, on both the long and short sides of the boards. Tap the boards immediately together using a mallet and tapping block. Fit the skirting boards.

35. You would expect the last piece of flooring to be laid in a right hand corner.

   True   False   Impossible to say

   Answer: [   ]

36. Starting the second row with the leftover piece will help ensure that adjoining end pieces are unaligned.

   True   False   Impossible to say

   Answer: [   ]

37. The short end of the board is its end.

True   False   Impossible to say

Answer: [   ]

Passage 13

It takes James nine minutes to get to the meeting, although he sets off five minutes later than Helen. It takes Steve longer to get to the meeting than Helen, but not as long as it takes James. It takes Pete and Sarah the same length of time to get to the meeting, but they do not set off at the same time. Sarah and James do set off at the same time. Steve and Pete arrive at the same time, just after Helen. Richard has to travel farther than anyone else.

38. It takes Steve nine minutes to travel to the meeting.

True   False   Impossible to say

Answer: [   ]

39. James arrives at the meeting after Helen.

True   False   Impossible to say

Answer: [   ]

40. Richard would have to set off before everyone else in order to arrive first.

True   False   Impossible to say

Answer: [   ]

Type B questions

Question 1

After a storm, the three main railway lines from Birmingham to London are all affected in different ways. The southern line is only running half its normal number of trains at their usual speed (although this is normally the slowest of the three services) but with all the trains scheduled to leave at five past each hour cancelled. The southeast line is running all its trains, but they are running at 50 per cent of their normal speed. The southwest line is also running all its trains, but is using an alternative route which adds 30 minutes to the journey time.

Which three additional pieces of information are required in order to work out which line will get to London earliest if a passenger is ready to leave Birmingham at 11.10 am?

1.   The southwest line has a train leaving at 11.15 am.
2.   The southeast line has a train leaving at 11.20 am.
3.   The southeast line is normally twice as fast as the southwest line.
4.   The southern line stops at more stations that either of the other lines.
5.   The southern line normally runs every half hour.
6.   The southwest line is a direct service.

Answer: _____

Question 2

Which of the following numbers complete the sequence:
   X, 9, 27, XX, 243, 729
1.   3
2.   8
3.   22
4.   64
5.   81

Answer: _____

Question 3

Robin commissioned an employment agency to fill a position in his company. The agency's fees are based on a percentage of the first year's remuneration. Which two pieces of information do you need to identify whether the final bill net of VAT of £3,750 is correct, given that the position was permanent, paid £20,000 a year with no other benefits, and that the candidate left the position after 10 weeks.

1. The bill is net of VAT, charged at 17.5 per cent.
2. Fixed term contracts are charged at an apportioned pro-rata basis of permanent fees.
3. If the employee leaves within 8 weeks of starting employment, a 50 per cent rebate applies. If the employee leaves between 9 and 12 weeks of the assignment, a 25 per cent rebate is provided.
4. If the remuneration includes the provision of a car, the sum of £2,000 shall be added to the first year's remuneration for purposes of calculating the introduction fee.
5. For annual remunerations up to £15,999 the introduction fee is 16 per cent, between £16,000 to £19,999 it is 20 per cent, and over £20,000 it is 25 per cent.

Answer: [   ]

Question 4

An American city is built around a grid of roads which run parallel and perpendicular to one another. Roads running north to south are labelled alphabetically, starting with 'A' in the west and 'Z' in the east. Roads running east to west are labelled numerically, starting with 1 in the south and 26 in the north. Starting on the junction of B and 4, I walk to the bookshop. On the way there I pass both the hospital and the cathedral. Which **one** additional item of information is required to locate the bookshop?

1.   The cathedral is on the junction of B and 7.
2.   The hospital in on the junction of G and 7.
3.   The cathedral is on the same north–south road as the bookshop.
4.   The bookshop is two blocks north and one block east of the junction of F and 8.
5.   The hospital is west of the bookshop.
6.   The bookshop is north of the cathedral.

Answer: [   ]

Question 5

An applicant to an industrial tribunal complained that she had received a lower percentage salary increase than some of her male colleagues. Evidence presented showed that she had received a 3 per cent increase, in line with most other employees. The employer provided explanations to demonstrate that the exceptions were all for good reason. Mr Smith had had a higher percentage increase to bring him up to the same salary as the applicant, and had been paid too little before that pay rise. Mr Gamble had received no pay rise at all because his recent review had found him to be ineffective in his post. Which piece of information best explains the tribunal's conclusion that the applicant's claim had failed?

1.   It is for the applicant to make out his or her case on the balance of probabilities.
2.   It is unusual to find direct evidence of sexual discrimination, and few employers will be prepared to admit such discrimination.
3.   The outcome of the case will therefore usually depend on what inferences it is proper to draw from the primary facts found by the tribunal.
4.   A finding of discrimination and a finding of a difference in gender will often point to the possibility of sexual discrimination. In such circumstances the tribunal will look to the employer for an explanation.

5.   At the conclusions of all the evidence the tribunal should reach a conclusion on the balance of probabilities bearing in mind the difficulties which face a person who complains of unlawful discrimination and the fact that it is for the complainant to provide his or her case.

Answer: [   ]

Question 6

George was 28 when his only son was born. Harry is George's elder brother and is 68 years older than George's granddaughter Sophie. Sophie's mother, whose father Dave is 52, is one year younger than her husband Peter and three years older than his cousin Simon. Which **two** additional pieces of information are required to determine how old George is?

1.   George is Simon's father.
2.   Peter is 35.
3.   Simon is Harry's nephew.
4.   Sophie is Simon's niece.
5.   Simon is younger than Dave.

Answer: [   ]

Question 7

A stakeholder pension is a simple and tax-efficient way of saving specifically for retirement. All contributions to a pension plan qualify for tax relief at the highest rate paid by the saver, and growth is free of UK income tax and capital gains tax. Savers are provided with their own plan and are sent regular statements showing the value of their fund. Fund prices are calculated daily. Management charges are due and calculated each day based on the value of the fund on that day. The fee is calculated at the beginning of each month and is based on 1/365th of the appropriate rate of the annual management fee.

Which piece(s) of information do you need in order to establish the level of management charges a stakeholder pension provider will make against a saver with a fund valued at £35,000?

1.   Stakeholder pension providers are allowed to charge a maximum annual management fee of 1 per cent of the fund value.
2.   Providers charge according to a tiered series of charges, with qualifying levels dependent on the saver's fund value.
3.   For funds valued up to £25,000 the fee is 1 per cent.
4.   For funds valued between £25,000 and £50,000 the fee is 0.8 per cent.
5.   For funds valued over £50,000 the fee is 0.6 per cent.

Answer:

Question 8
Which **one** piece of information is a satisfactory schema for the logical truth that Brutus killed Caesar or Brutus did not kill Caesar.

1.   If p then q.
2.   P and Q.
3.   If x then y.
4.   p or not p.

Answer:

Question 9
Every organization requires working capital in order that the company can hold sufficient stock, allow its customers some credit, and pay its suppliers when payments become due. A working capital ratio is used to measure the relationship between current assets and current liabilities. An often accepted

ratio is about 2:1, where the value of assets is twice as much as the value of liabilities. Which **three** pieces of information are required in order to identify the working capital ratio for a retail outlet?

1. Value of assets £50,000.
2. Bank account balance £23,000 in credit.
3. Net profit £100,000.
4. Debtors £14,000.
5. Corporation tax paid £14,000.

Answer: _____

Question 10
Which of the following numbers complete the sequence:
    1, 8, 27, 64, XXX, XXX
1. 243
2. 120
3. 250
4. 125
5. 216

Answer: _____

Question 11
If the Earth is flat and its ends are not visible from where you are standing, then a ship sailing from a port in a straight line should appear to get smaller and smaller until it disappears. Which of the following statements proves this flat Earth hypothesis as false:

1. When a ship can no longer be seen with the naked eye, a telescope will allow the observer to see it once again. The ends of the Earth therefore cannot be invisible.

2. A ship when observed to sail in a straight line away from the observer appears to sink away rather than only become smaller.
3. If the world were flat then a ship would still fall off the edge, if that event was unobserved.
4. If the world were flat then the ship must at some point be seen to fall off the edge.
5. A ship when it sails away from a port is observed from the shore to get smaller and smaller.

Answer: [   ]

Question 12
Which of the following numbers complete the sequence:

　1, 2, X, 5, 7, 11, XX, 17, 19, XX, 29

1. 3
2. 22
3. 13
4. 14
5. 23

Answer: [   ]

Fast Stream Mock Tests

This chapter comprises mock tests for the Fast Stream. Use them to practise under realistic conditions, and approach them as if they were for real. Remember that to show your true potential, you really have to go for it and apply yourself. Make this kind of commitment under practice conditions as well as in the real test, then you will be able to perfect your exam technique and maximize the benefit of practice.

Mock test 1: verbal test

This test comprises 16 questions. Allow yourself 10 minutes to complete it. The question layout and answer box is of the same style as found in the real test.

1

A We use numbers when shopping, or at home when cooking or gardening. **B** Tradesmen, shopkeepers, accountants, scientists, engineers, architects and many others all use numbers in their work. **C** Arithmetic is the branch of mathematics concerned with numbers. **D** It is one of the most useful branches, since numbers are used by almost everybody.

	1st	2nd	3rd	4th
A				
B				
C				
D				

2

A Arsine, a colourless, poisonous gas compound of arsenic and hydrogen, is used as a doping agent for semiconductors and as a military poison gas. **B** The compounds of arsenic are mostly poisonous. **C** Among the most important commercially are arsenious oxide (white arsenic), used in pesticides and in the manufacture of glass and the preserving of animal hides, and arsenic pentoxide, which supplies a major ingredient in the production of insecticides, herbicides and weedkillers, and metal adhesives. **D** Arsenic acid, lead arsenate, and calcium arsenate are all important in agriculture in sterilizing soils and controlling pests.

	1st	2nd	3rd	4th
A				
B				
C				
D				

3

A When the wax is removed, only the areas that were not waxed are coloured. **B** The cloth is then dyed and dried. **C** Instead of painting or printing a colour directly on a cloth, as in most patterned fabrics, the worker covers parts of the fabric with wax. **D** The process used for batik is called resist dyeing.

	1st	2nd	3rd	4th
A				
B				
C				
D				

4
A Friction comes from the Latin word meaning 'rub'. **B** Friction always occurs when two articles are moved so as to rub or chafe against one another. **C** This resistance, or force which opposes motion, is called friction. **D** When a heavy wooden box is pushed along the floor, resistance is set up between the box and the floor.

	1st	2nd	3rd	4th
A				
B				
C				
D				

5
A The eel-like hagfish has a very unpleasant way of life. **B** Over 100 hagfish have been found in one large, dead fish. **C** If the 'host' fish was alive originally, it slowly dies as its body is eaten away. **D** It bores its way into the bodies of other fish – alive, dead or dying – and burrows through their flesh, eating as it goes.

	1st	2nd	3rd	4th
A				
B				
C				
D				

6
A The laws were written in the Sumerian language, in wedge-shaped letters called cruciform. **B** Hammurabi, a wise and able ruler, was concerned with bringing order and justice to his kingdom. **C** This was a collection of more than 280 laws, which he had inscribed on a great stone pillar. **D** He set up a strong central government and gathered all the laws of his kingdom into a great code.

	1st	2nd	3rd	4th
A				
B				
C				
D				

7
A (Australia, though larger, is not usually counted as an island.) **B** More than four-fifths of its area consists of a vast ice cap rising very gradually to a central dome, and only in the

coastal regions can people live or plants grow.   **C**   Greenland is about 2,670 km from north to south, and over 1,050 km at its widest point east to west.   **D**   Greenland is the world's largest island and is located in the north Atlantic Ocean, off the east coast of Canada.

	1ˢᵗ	2ⁿᵈ	3ʳᵈ	4ᵗʰ
A				
B				
C				.
D				

8

A   A standard medicine such as paracetamol (acetaminophen) may help to lower or relieve aches and pains, though it won't alter the course of the illness.   **B**   Whooping cough and some of the other infections are caused by bacteria, in which case drugs may often help to fight the illness.   **C**   Chickenpox, measles, German measles, and mumps are all caused by viruses. **D**   Few drugs are effective against viruses and so the best treatment is to let the patient rest, as his or her body attacks and kills the viruses naturally.

	1ˢᵗ	2ⁿᵈ	3ʳᵈ	4ᵗʰ
A				
B				
C				
D				

9

A   With it, it is possible to build dams, foundations, tall slender bridges, high-rise buildings, and paved areas such as roads and airfield runways.   **B**   Cement is used in one of several ways in nearly every building in the western world, and hundreds of millions of tonnes of cement are used throughout the world every year.   **C**   Cement is one of the most versatile binders known to man.   **D**   It is also used in the manufacture of building blocks, roofing tiles, and even things as thin as roofing sheet.

	1ˢᵗ	2ⁿᵈ	3ʳᵈ	4ᵗʰ
A				
B				
C				
D				

10
A   This is doubtful.   **B**   Paintings made in the first half of the 18th century show the members of one clan in different tartans, and even one clansman with separate tartans for his coat, waistcoat and kilt, and it is unlikely that the clans kept strictly to particular tartans until the 19th century.   **C**   The oldest known painting showing Highland dress dates from about 1660, and few earlier records are reliable.   **D**   It is sometimes claimed that the different Scottish tartans served in ancient times to distinguish not only the different clans but also the ranks of the clansmen.

	1st	2nd	3rd	4th
A				
B				
C				
D				

11
A   The body of the common African civet is about 90 cm long, a little less than the length of its bushy tail.   **B**   The coarse grey fur is tinged with yellow and marked with black spots and bands.   **C**   As a rule the civet lives in a hole in the ground, coming out mostly at night to search for rodents, birds, and insects; it will also eat fruit.   **D**   The civets of India and other parts of Asia, of which there are several kinds, are usually smaller and their fur is striped rather than spotted.

	1st	2nd	3rd	4th
A				
B				
C				
D				

12
A   Nowadays, many people camp without 'roughing it', using caravans, campers or tents with all the modern comforts of home: a cooker, shower, toilet and even a television.   **B**   Tents have been used by people for thousands of years.   **C**   Explorers and mountain climbers have camped in some of the

most remote and unfriendly places on Earth.   D   They are still the chief homes for some, such as the wandering Bedouin of North Africa and Arabia.

	1st	2nd	3rd	4th
A				
B				
C				
D				

13

A   Slow-speed film (50 ASA or less) reacts slowly to light and is used in very bright conditions, such as sun or snow.   B   Film comes in different 'speeds', given on the packet in ASA/ISO or DIN numbers.   C   The light passing through the lens of a camera acts on the light-sensitive chemicals in the film, which, after being developed (or processed), produces a negative from which prints can be made.   D   Medium-speed film (50 to 125 ASA) is for normal sunny conditions, and fast-speed film (200–400 ASA) is best for cloudy or dim conditions.

	1st	2nd	3rd	4th
A				
B				
C				
D				

14

A   The state has been made habitable by water, natural gas, and hydroelectric power, mostly brought in from the outside, and by the invention of air conditioning.   B   Most of its landscape consists of rugged mountains, arid desert, mesas and buttes.   C   More than 300 ranges of mountains cross the state north to south.   D   Nevada is the driest state in the United States of America and one of the hottest.

	1st	2nd	3rd	4th
A				
B				
C				
D				

15
A At intervals along the mycelium fruiting bodies, or sporophores, develop. **B** Mushrooms spread by spores that develop on the gills. **C** These grow into a massive network of underground threads (mycelium). **D** When the spores ripen they are released, and if they land in a warm moist place they grow into thread-like chains of cells (hyphae).

	1st	2nd	3rd	4th
A				
B				
C				
D				

16
A Some people are born with greater possibilities or 'potential intelligence' than others. **B** Intelligence is improved by learning. **C** It is no longer thought that intelligence is a general quality, underlying all behaviour and inherited wholly from our parents. **D** However, this potential may not develop unless it is encouraged and stimulated by influences surrounding the child from birth.

	1st	2nd	3rd	4th
A				
B				
C				
D				

End of test.

Mock test 2: quantitative reasoning, easy to medium-hard questions

This test comprises 20 questions. Allow yourself 30 minutes to complete it. Shade the boxes alongside each unit of the answer: for example record 5 as 005.

1

A	B	C
4	15	59
12	9	107
17	19	322
3	3	8
12	14	?

0	0	0
1	1	1
2	2	2
3	3	3
4	4	4
5	5	5
6	6	6
7	7	7
8	8	8
9	9	9

2

A	B	C
12	14	167
4	19	75
19	13	246
17	12	203
12	44	?

0	0	0
1	1	1
2	2	2
3	3	3
4	4	4
5	5	5
6	6	6
7	7	7
8	8	8
9	9	9

3

A	B	C
12	3	0
18	14	38
10	20	70
11	13	41
52	100	?

0	0	0
1	1	1
2	2	2
3	3	3
4	4	4
5	5	5
6	6	6
7	7	7
8	8	8
9	9	9

4

A	B	C
72	40	88
13	23	79
54	14	2
23	23	69
10	40	?

0	0	0
1	1	1
2	2	2
3	3	3
4	4	4
5	5	5
6	6	6
7	7	7
8	8	8
9	9	9

5

A	B	C
42	13	10
112	112	336
14	54	202
72	72	216
39	49	?

0	0	0
1	1	1
2	2	2
3	3	3
4	4	4
5	5	5
6	6	6
7	7	7
8	8	8
9	9	9

6

A	B	C
3	7	22
3	9	24
2	3	13
6	12	42
4	1	?

0	0	0
1	1	1
2	2	2
3	3	3
4	4	4
5	5	5
6	6	6
7	7	7
8	8	8
9	9	9

7

A	B	C
7	3	38
9	32	77
17	81	166
22	12	122
30	10	?

0	0	0
1	1	1
2	2	2
3	3	3
4	4	4
5	5	5
6	6	6
7	7	7
8	8	8
9	9	9

8

A	B	C
12	4	64
44	1	221
3	3	18
7	5	40
13	13	?

0	0	0
1	1	1
2	2	2
3	3	3
4	4	4
5	5	5
6	6	6
7	7	7
8	8	8
9	9	9

9

A	B	C
12	2	16
14	3	23
2	2	6
4	4	20
5	3	?

0	0	0
1	1	1
2	2	2
3	3	3
4	4	4
5	5	5
6	6	6
7	7	7
8	8	8
9	9	9

10

A	B	C
10	12	154
10	14	206
14	16	270
14	18	338
18	20	?

0	0	0
1	1	1
2	2	2
3	3	3
4	4	4
5	5	5
6	6	6
7	7	7
8	8	8
9	9	9

11

A	B	C
90	90	8190
12	1	13
10	10	110
15	15	240
1	12	?

0	0	0
1	1	1
2	2	2
3	3	3
4	4	4
5	5	5
6	6	6
7	7	7
8	8	8
9	9	9

12

A	B	C
4	4	12
3	2	7
5	3	22
9	5	76
6	2	?

0	0	0
1	1	1
2	2	2
3	3	3
4	4	4
5	5	5
6	6	6
7	7	7
8	8	8
9	9	9

13

A	B	C
1	0.5	0.5
12	72	72
10	4.8	95.2
5	5	20
3	1.2	?

0	0	0.0
1	1	0.1
2	2	0.2
3	3	0.3
4	4	0.4
5	5	0.5
6	6	0.6
7	7	0.7
8	8	0.8
9	9	0.9

14

A	B	C
29	14	827
25	12	613
22	100	384
18	200	124
14	150	?

0	0	0
1	1	1
2	2	2
3	3	3
4	4	4
5	5	5
6	6	6
7	7	7
8	8	8
9	9	9

15

A	B	C
3	2	13
4	2	20
1	1	2
3	3	18
4	4	?

0	0	0
1	1	1
2	2	2
3	3	3
4	4	4
5	5	5
6	6	6
7	7	7
8	8	8
9	9	9

16

A	B	C
16	12	400
5	5	50
12	1	145
4	4	32
9	6	?

0	0	0
1	1	1
2	2	2
3	3	3
4	4	4
5	5	5
6	6	6
7	7	7
8	8	8
9	9	9

17

A	B	C
25	20	1025
10	15	325
10	10	200
15	15	450
20	10	?

0	0	0
1	1	1
2	2	2
3	3	3
4	4	4
5	5	5
6	6	6
7	7	7
8	8	8
9	9	9

18

A	B	C
4	1	1
49	2	5
100	4	6
121	3	8
16	4	?

0	0	0
1	1	1
2	2	2
3	3	3
4	4	4
5	5	5
6	6	6
7	7	7
8	8	8
9	9	9

19

A	B	C
196	12	2
64	0	8
121	10.1	0.9
289	12	5
10000	91.2	?

0	0	0.0
1	1	0.1
2	2	0.2
3	3	0.3
4	4	0.4
5	5	0.5
6	6	0.6
7	7	0.7
8	8	0.8
9	9	0.9

20

A	B	C
36	4	2
64	5	3
144	10	2
625	14	11
1600	12	?

0	0	0
1	1	1
2	2	2
3	3	3
4	4	4
5	5	5
6	6	6
7	7	7
8	8	8
9	9	9

End of test.

Mock test 3: more practice for the verbal test

This test comprises 15 questions. Allow yourself 15 minutes to complete it.

1

A This usually amounts to about £16,000. **B** Even so, some former MPs struggle to make ends meet. **C** On top of this, they receive a 'winding-up' allowance to take care of any unpaid staff, and research or other expenses. **D** MPs do get golden handshakes and they are fairly generous, with payments of between 50 and 100 per cent of their annual £55,118 salary given to them when the electorate turns nasty.

	1st	2nd	3rd	4th
A				
B				
C				
D				

2

A These include, for example, the use of diamonds in a dentist's drill. **B** The remainder are used for industrial purposes, that is, for useful as distinct from decorative purposes. **C** Other applications of industrial diamonds are found in engineering, where tools with very hard surfaces are needed for cutting and grinding other hard surfaces. **D** Less than 50 per cent of rough diamonds are suitable for cutting and turning into jewellery.

	1st	2nd	3rd	4th
A				
B				
C				
D				

3

A Slowly, differences in ways of speaking become more and more marked, and these differences will eventually make a new dialect. **B** Dialects come about when people who have been living together and speaking to one another in the same way move apart. **C** Language changes, even as it is passed on from parents to children. **D** Separation of groups of people by a move across a physical barrier, such as a mountain or a river, can lead to different ways of speaking the same language.

	1st	2nd	3rd	4th
A				
B				
C				
D				

4
A The amount of work performed to bring about an energy change is exactly equal to the quantity of energy being converted into new forms.   **B**   The total energy at the end of any change is the same as the total energy before the change. **C** This is an important principle known as the conservation of energy.   **D**   Energy may be changed from one form to another, and work is the process that brings about the change.

	1st	2nd	3rd	4th
A				
B				
C				
D				

5
A Many of them reproduce so slowly that they are unable to make up for the numbers that are wiped out.   **B**   It is thought that one species becomes extinct every day, while many more become threatened.   **C**   Biologists estimate that 1 in 10 of all species are in danger of dying out.   **D**   That means there are at least a million endangered species of plants and animals.

	1st	2nd	3rd	4th
A				
B				
C				
D				

6
A Sometimes they are based on time – the worker being paid at a rate of so much an hour or so much a week; and sometimes they are based on articles produced – a shirtmaker, for example, being paid at a rate of so much for every shirt made (piece work). **B** Payments of this type are usually controlled by law, so that the worker is protected against a bad employer who might try to pay all or nearly all his wages in kind.   **C** Wages, or salaries, are payments by employers to their employees in return for work.   **D** Wages are paid in money, but sometimes they include payments in kind, as when a caretaker is provided with a rent-free house and miners are given free or very cheap coal.

	1st	2nd	3rd	4th
A				
B				
C				
D				

7

A Throughout the world, techniques to measure pupil development and achievement have improved in recent years. **B** Standardized tests are used to a great extent. **C** These serve not only to compare a student with his or her fellow classmates but also to compare him or her with other students in the country at large. **D** The emphasis on individual differences and pupil interests has led to better methods of assessment.

	1st	2nd	3rd	4th
A				
B				
C				
D				

8

A This is known as the circular flow of income. **B** In economic life people are dependent on each other. **C** Whenever somebody spends, somebody else earns. **D** Macroeconomics is the study of how the whole of a country's economy works.

	1st	2nd	3rd	4th
A				
B				
C				
D				

9

A In fact the word echinoderm means 'spiny-skinned'. **B** In sea urchins this is very obvious. **C** In many echinoderms these plates have knobs or spines on them which stick through the skin and give the creature a prickly appearance. **D** The skeleton is made of hard, chalky plates just under the skin.

	1st	2nd	3rd	4th
A				
B				
C				
D				

10

A The oceanic crust is only 6–8 km thick. **B** There are two kinds of crust. **C** The continental crust averages 35 km, but reaches a thickness of 60–70 km under high mountain ranges. **D** One kind, the 'oceanic crust', is beneath the oceans and

seas, while the other, the 'continental crust', composes the
continents.

	1st	2nd	3rd	4th
A				
B				
C				
D				

11

A   Sound waves can neither be seen nor be felt, but the ear is so
delicate that it catches all the shades of difference in them.   **B**
Only when they reach the brain do we hear anything.   **C**   The
hammer, anvil and stirrup of the middle ear take up the vibra-
tions, magnify them, and pass them on through the fluid of the
cochlea to the nerve endings of the inner ear and so to the brain.
D   A sound is first caught by that part of the ear that is outside
the head and is then sent down the canal to the ear-drum,
making it vibrate.

	1st	2nd	3rd	4th
A				
B				
C				
D				

12

A   Dyslexia tends to run in families, and is more common in
males than females.   **B**   Most dyslexics also have problems
with spelling.   **C**   People with dyslexia have trouble seeing the
differences between words, and will often misread them.   **D**
They may reverse the letters in a word, for example, substi-
tuting saw for was, or find substitutes for the printed word, so
that hot may be read as pot.

	1st	2nd	3rd	4th
A				
B				
C				
D				

13

A   The men wore plain linen collars, jerkins, and breeches, and
had   short   hair   (which   earned   them   the   nickname
'Roundheads'), while the women chose dark, plain dress styles.
B   The Royalist side continued to wear elegant court satins,

plumed hats and, even for men, long ringleted hair styles.   **C**
An important development in the middle of the 17th century
was that clothing became an obvious symbol of the religious
and political differences that split England during the Civil War.
D   The Parliamentary forces, who were Puritans, adopted very
plain clothes.

	1st	2nd	3rd	4th
A				
B				
C				
D				

14

A   It may have as many as 40 or 50 buckets, each capable of
raising 1 cubic metre of spoil.   **B**   A dredger of this kind will
easily raise 40,000 cubic metres of spoil in a week.   **C**   A
bucket dredger is a particularly useful machine because it can
dredge quite accurately to a required depth and leaves the
ground over which it has worked fairly level.   **D**   If the
cutting edges of the buckets are fitted with teeth the dredger can
even cut and raise soft rock.

	1st	2nd	3rd	4th
A				
B				
C				
D				

15

A   If, however, there is an opposing piece in the next black
square, and an empty black square beyond it, then that piece
may be captured and removed from the board by jumping over
it.   **B**   Black always has the first move.   **C**   Sometimes
several pieces can be taken like this in a single row and the
winner is the player who either captures all his opponent's
pieces or blocks them so that they cannot move.   **D**   A move
is made by advancing a piece diagonally forward into an empty
black square touching the one it is currently in.

End of test.

	1st	2nd	3rd	4th
A				
B				
C				
D				

Mock test 4: data interpretation

This test comprises 16 questions. Allow yourself 20 minutes to complete it.

Addison, Baldock, Clark, Dickinson, Edwards, Fitch, Gordon, Humphreys, Isaacs, Jordan, Keith, Lloyd, Milton, Newton and Orwell all take extra woodwind lessons on a Tuesday. Using their initials, Mrs Richards, their peripatetic teacher, has produced the following monthly timetable (Table 5.1):

Each child pays £5.00 per lesson, unless they are subsidized by the school, then they pay £2.50. Addison, Dickinson, Edwards,

Table 5.1   Monthly timetable

Date	5/11	12/11	19/11	26/11
08.30	A	H	F	N
09.00	O	I	K	D
09.30	C	A	H	F
10.00	M	O	I	K
10.30	E	C	A	H
11.00	L	M	O	I
11.30	G	E	C	A
12.00	J	L	M	O
12.30	B	G	E	C
13.00	N	J	L	M
13.30	D	B	G	E
14.00	F	N	J	L
14.30	K	D	B	G
15.00	H	F	N	J
15.30	I	K	D	B

Fitch and Keith are currently subsidized, although Addison and Edwards will begin paying full rate from 14 November.

1. On average, which are Mrs Richards' most profitable
    lessons?

    A 08.30; 09.00; 10.00; 11.00
    B 09.30; 10.00; 12.00; 12.30
    C 11.00; 12.00; 12.30; 13.00
    D 13.30; 14.00; 15.00; 15.30

    Answer: [   ]

2. When it comes near to examination time Mrs Richards
    offers extra tuition after school at £6.00 per half hour, or
    £3.50 each if a shared lesson is used. Music exams start in
    December. Clark, Gordon and Humphreys have requested
    extra lessons. Clark and Gordon both play the saxophone
    and will share their lesson. Extra tuition starts on 19
    November. How much money will Mrs Richards be
    earning for this week?

    A £75.50   B £80.50   C £81.50   D £83.50

    Answer: [   ]

3. Due to sickness among many of her students, Mrs
    Richards has to reorganize her timetable for the week of
    26 November. The altered lessons are as follows: Edwards
    at 14.30; Gordon at 10.00; Jordan at 12.00; Keith at
    11.00; and Orwell at 13.30. Baldock and Isaacs are away
    sick. From 13.00 her appointments are as follows:

    A M A K E
    B M I K E
    C M O C K E D
    D M O L E

    Answer: [   ]

4.   The school concert is planned for 22 December. Every
     student is given five tickets at £4.00 each to sell to friends
     and family. £212.00 and a number of unsold tickets are
     returned. Jordan did not sell any, whereas Addison,
     Dickinson, Fitch, Keith, Lloyd and Newton sold all theirs.
     What is the average number of tickets sold per student?

     A 2.80   B 3.00   C 3.50   D 4.00

                          Answer: [   ]

InterSun Ltd has slashed the price of holidays to the Canary
Islands. In Table 5.2 their new rates are shown compared with
their old fares:

Table 5.2   InterSun Ltd holidays

| Departure dates | | Destination | Board | Price per person/week | |
From	To			Old	New
1 July	14 July	Fuerteventura	SC	£150	£125
		Gran Canaria	SC	£165	£130
		Lanzarote	HB	£180	£140
		Tenerife	HB	£200	£150
15 July	28 July	Fuerteventura	SC	£200	£150
		Gran Canaria	SC	£215	£160
		Lanzarote	HB	£230	£180
		Tenerife	HB	£250	£200
29 July	31 August	Fuerteventura	SC	£250	£200
		Gran Canaria	SC	£275	£225
		Lanzarote	HB	£325	£275
		Tenerife	HB	£350	£300

5. A customer wants to visit Lanzarote for two weeks between 7 and 21 July. How much will he or she save?

    A £80   B £90   C £100   D £110

    Answer: [   ]

6. Airport tax increases on 10 August to £65.00 per person, from an original £42.00 per person. InterSun Ltd has already sold 6731 holidays for this period and cannot now introduce the new charge to these customers. What are its losses?

    A £154,813   B £154,956   C £164,765   D £165,814

    Answer: [   ]

7. Self Catering (SC) holidays offer a further 25 per cent reduction on prices for holidays in Fuerteventura during August. What is the total saving on the original price for a two-week holiday starting 21 July?

    A £187.50   B £175.00   C £160.50   D £150.00

    Answer: [   ]

8. In August, which destination has the greatest percentage increase over the late July fares?

    A Fuerteventura   B Gran Canaria   C Lanzarote
    D Tenerife

    Answer: [   ]

Kash Ltd offer Personal Loans at 8.9 per cent APR*. Table 5.3 below shows the repayments over various monthly instalments either with Payment Protection Cover (PP) or without Payment Protection Cover (W/O) for loans between £5,000 and £20,000. Payment Protection Cover ensures continued loan repayments in the event of involuntary unemployment, illness or disability. All repayments are fixed for the entire period of the loan and guaranteed never to rise.

Table 5.3   Kash Ltd

| Loan | 12 months | | 24 months | | 36 months | | 48 months | | 60 months | |
£	W/O	PP	W/O	PP	W/O	PP	W/O	PP	W/O	PP
20,000	1745.26	1865.77	909.97	999.94	632.22	704.25	793.85	569.86	411.23	482.21
17,500	1527.10	1632.55	796.22	875.03	553.19	616.22	432.12	498.63	359.83	421.94
15,000	1308.95	1399.33	682.48	750.03	474.16	528.19	371.39	427.40	308.42	361.65
12,500	1090.79	1166.11	568.73	625.02	395.14	440.16	308.65	356.16	257.02	301.38
10,000	872.63	932.89	454.98	500.01	316.11	352.13	246.92	284.93	205.62	241.11
8,000	698.10	746.30	363.99	400.02	252.89	281.70	197.54	227.95	164.49	192.88
6,000	523.58	559.73	272.99	300.01	189.66	211.27	148.15	170.95	123.37	144.66
5,000	436.32	466.45	227.49	250.01	158.05	176.06	123.46	142.46	102.81	120.55

*Customers who do not satisfy Kash Ltd's normal scoring criteria may be offered a loan with an APR of up to 4 per cent above the typical rates shown. An additional variable administration fee will also be payable; information concerning that is available upon request.

9.   How much will a customer repay Kash Ltd for a loan of £12,500 borrowed over 48 months (with Payment Protection Cover)?

A £13,676.64   B £14,815.20   C £15,421.20
D £17,095.68   E £18,505.20   F £20,515.20

Answer:

10. Kash Ltd offers a repayment plan of £154.21 over 60 months for a loan of £7,500. This is a saving of £598.80 on a competitor, Loans-R-Us Ltd, who offer their customers an APR of 11.9 per cent over the same period. How much in total do customers of Loans-R-Us Ltd repay?

    A £8,098.80   B £9,252.60   C £9,851.40
    D £9,993.50   E £10,156.00   F £10,512.80

    Answer: [   ]

11. Mr Patel requests a loan for £10,000. Which of the following is his cheapest form of repayment?

    A 12 months PP   B 24 months W/O   C 24 months PP
    D 36 months W/O   E 36 months PP   F 48 months W/O

    Answer: [   ]

12. Unfortunately Mr Fox has a very poor credit rating and Kash Ltd has offered him an APR 3 per cent above the typical rate for a loan of £5,000. What are his monthly repayments (without Payment Protection Cover) over 36 months?

    A 164.40   B 176.06   C 185.45   D 187.60   E 191.23
    F Cannot be calculated

    Answer: [   ]

Table 5.4 shows the high and low tides at Liverpool for one week during April. Information is provided for the time of the tide, its height, and the sun and moon times. Note: all times shown are GMT.

Table 5.4   Liverpool tides

Date	High water				Low water				Sun		Moon	
	Morning		Afternoon		Morning		Afternoon		Rise	Set	Rise	Set
	Time	m	Time	m	Time	m	Time	m				
14.04	0001	9.2	1216	9.3	0634	1.1	1853	1.0	0530	1856	1933	0229
15.04	0030	9.1	1247	9.2	0707	1.1	1924	1.1	0527	1858	2046	0304
16.04	0100	9.0	1318	9.0	0741	1.3	1956	1.4	0525	1859	2144	0350
17.04	0131	8.8	1350	8.7	0814	1.6	2028	1.8	0523	1901	2228	0450
18.04	0203	8.5	1428	8.3	0848	2.0	2102	2.3	0520	1903	2259	0558
19.04	0242	8.1	1516	7.9	0927	2.4	2144	2.7	0518	1905	2323	0712
20.04	0337	7.7	1624	7.4	1022	2.8	2249	3.1	0516	1907	2341	0826

13.   What is the range in tide height throughout the week?

A 1.0m   B 7.7m   C 8.1m   D 8.3m   E 9.2m   F 9.3m

Answer: [   ]

14.   Which period has the lowest mean tide?

A Morning   B Afternoon   C Both the same
D Cannot be calculated

Answer: [   ]

15.   How many hours of sunlight is there on 17 April?

A 14hr 38m   B 14hr 28m   C 14hr 18m
D 13hr 78m   E 13hr 58m   F 13hr 38m

Answer: [   ]

16. Southport lies 35 minutes behind Liverpool. What time was the morning high tide at Southport on 14 April?

A There was no morning tide   B 0026   C 0036
D 1126   E 1141   F 1226

Answer: [   ]

End of test.

Answers and Explanations

Answers and explanations to Chapter 2

Handling data: the essentials

1. East
   Explanation: All you need to do to answer this type of question is to know the points of the compass and know the directions of clockwise and anticlockwise. Try drawing it out on a piece of paper if you did not get the right answer.
2. West
3. North
4. No
   Explanation: David could have made his turns in either direction in order to end up facing East.
5. 75p
   Explanation: 3.00 divided by 4 = 75p.
6. 28
   Explanation: £21 divided by £3 = 7 packs purchased. Multiply by 4 batteries per pack = 28 batteries.

7.   £5.32
     Explanation: 1.33 multiplied by 4 = £5.32.
8.   £18
     Explanation: £1.50 multiplied by 12 = £18.
9.   16
     Explanation: 48 divided by 3 = 16.
10. £6.24
     Explanation: Four boxes of eggs are needed. £1.56 multiplied by 4 = £6.24.
11. £5.20
     Explanation: The price of an egg is £1.56 divided by 6 = 26p. Multiply by 20 = £5.20.
12. 360 gm
     Explanation: 6 multiplied by 60 = 360.
13. 200 gm
     Explanation: Weight of one egg is 300 gm divided by 6 = 50 gm. Multiply by 4 = 200 gm.
14. 11
     Explanation: £132 divided by 12 = 11.
15. 40
     Explanation: Divide 1200 (p) by 30 (p) = 40.
16   £8.80
     Explanation: 16 multiplied by 0.55 = 8.8.
17. 0.25 gm
     Explanation: 400 divided by 1600 = 0.25.
18. 111 gm
     Explanation: There are 37 x 10 = 370 beans. Multiply by the weight of each: 370 x 0.3 = 111 gm.
19. £7.00
     Explanation: 25 multiplied by 28 = 700 pence or £7.00.
20. £66.66
     Explanation: 10.1 multiplied by 660 = 6666 pence or £66.66.
21. £2.40
     Explanation: 48 x 5% = 2.4.
22. 12
     Explanation: 100% = 60, 10% = 6 so 20% = 12.

23. 80
     Explanation: 60 minutes divided by 3 = 20 buses per hour.
     Multiply by 4 = 80 per shift.

24. 12 minutes
     Explanation: 6 hours consists of 360 minutes which
     divided by 30 = 12.

25. 33.3%
     Explanation: 13 is a third of 39 or 33.3%

26. 7 minutes and 30 seconds
     Explanation: 45 multiplied by 10 = 450 seconds. Divided
     by 60 to convert to minutes, = 7.5 or 7 minutes 30
     seconds.

27. £22.50
     Explanation: 202.50 divided by 9 = 22.50.

28. £60
     Explanation: 4 multiplied by 30 = 120 divided by 2 = 60.

29. £13.44

30. Yes
     Explanation: The total VAT cost will be £2100 which is
     17.5% of £12,000.

31. 27

32. Yes
     Explanation: 17.5% of 1,500,000 = 262,500.

33. 1,125 ml

34. 3.25 pm

35. €30.6

36. More than
     Explanation: The vendor would receive about £326,000.

37. 90
     Explanation: Each litter of 9 multiplied by the 9 piglets =
     81 to which you must add the original 9 piglets giving you
     90.

38. 3%
     Explanation: A 1% increase is 5.3 schools so an increase
     of 16 is equal to just over 3%.

Quantitative reasoning

1. C

    Multiply the price of one dozen by 3.5: 1.2 x 3.5 = 4.2.

2. D

    To calculate the weight of a single parcel, divide the weight
    of two parcels by two: 0.5/2 = 0.25 kg. Take away the
    weight of a parcel from the combined weight of a parcel
    and a letter to get the weight of a letter 0.35 − 0.25 = 0.1.
    Multiply by two for the weight of two letters: 0.1 x 2 = 0.2.

3. B

    One third of the full price is 33.33%. The remainder is
    66.66%, so the discount was 66.66%.

4. F

    One quarter of £24,840 is £6210. Add that quarter to the
    year 2000 profit: £24,840 + £6210 = £31,050.

5. B

    64 − 25% = 48 and 16 − 25% = 12.

6. D

    277,000 − 67,000 − 21,000 − 103,000 = 86,000

7. D

    One coach can accommodate 75/3 = 25 passengers. Divide
    150 by 25 = 6.

8. A

    Divide the total income by the number of people:
    11340/126 = 9.

9. D

    Sophie spends 1.30 h travelling each way, equals 3 h every
    day. She works 5 days per week so 3 x 5 = 15.

10. E

    Add up all the overtime hours: 2 + 1.5 + 1 + 2.5 + 3 = 10,
    then divide by the number of staff: 10/5 = 2.

11. D

    £70 + 5% = £73.50 and £80 − 45% =£ 44. £73.50 + £44 =
    £117.50 per week.

12. F
     Multiply the number of coins by the fraction of a pound
     the coin represents: (7 x 1/2 = £3.50) + (18 x 1/5 = £3.60)
     + (33 x 1/10 = £3.30) + (12 x 1/20 = £0.60) + (15 x 1/50 =
     £0.30) = £11.30.

13. F
     We can calculate the number of self-employed staff by
     finding out the percentage 29 members of staff represent.
     The remaining 24% + 18% = 42%, therefore 29 = 58%.
     By dividing 29 by 58% we can find out 1%: 29/58 = 0.5 of
     a member of staff. By multiplying 24% by 0.5 we find out
     the number of self-employed staff = 12.

14. D
     The ratio of investment between B and A is 1:2.5,
     therefore the total investment = 3.5. Divide £70,000 by 3.5
     = £20,000 = 1 = B's contribution.

15. C
     Divide the copies per machine per hour by 60 minutes:
     180/60 = 3 copies per minute. One photocopier can
     produce 3 x 25 = 75 copies in 25 minutes. Two photo-
     copiers can produce twice as much = 150 copies.

16. A
     Angela spends 35 hours per week in the office (7 h x 5
     days). Divide by 7 and multiply by 3: (35/7) * 3 = 15 hours
     per week typing letters.

17. C
     12 m x 18.5 m = 222 sq m x £2.25 = £499.50.

18. F
     £64 as a percentage of 400 is 64/400 x 100 = 16%.

19. D
     Calculate the actual length in cm by multiplying 57.5 by
     2000 = 115,000 cm. To convert to metres, divide by 100:
     115,000/100 = 1,150 m.

20. C
     There are 3.5 times more female than male workers. 4 x
     3.5 = 14.

21. D
   The total amount needed for the trip is €400 x 4 days = €1,600.To covert to Sterling, divide by the exchange rate: 1,600/1.6 = £1000.

22. A
   John and Sarah together earn £46,700 (18,700 +28,000). Mark earns 53% of this amount (47% less than John and Sarah). 1% = £457; 53% = £24,751.

23. B
   2000: £1,250 x 110% = £1,375. 2001: £1,375 x 110% = £1,512.50.

24. A
   Divide the total number of employees by the sum of the ratio: 370/10 = 37. Multiply by the 7 old: = 259.

25. C
   The annual target is 150 sales x 4 quarters = 600. Average 137 per quarter x 3 quarters = 411. 600 – 411 = 189.

26. A
   The £15,400 equals 100% minus 23% of the secretary's income = 77%. Her full income is 15400/77*100 = £20,000.

27. E
   First we need to find out how many people Company A employs. If Company C employs 25% less than A then 120 = 75%; 120/75 = 1.6 x 100 = 160. Therefore, Company A employs 160 people. Ratio A to B is 2:1 so Company B employs 160/2 = 80 people.

28. B
   The office area is 11 m x 12.5 m = 137.5 sq m. Deduct the area underneath the cabinet: 125 cm x 80 cm = 10,000 sq cm which converts to 1 sq m, so the area to be carpeted is 136.5 sq m. Four tiles 50 cm by 50 cm are required to carpet each sq m, so the total needed is 136.5 x 4 = 546.

29. E
   £3,700 – 35% = £2,405. The amount of this proportion spent is 3/12 on the speaker and 8/12 on the transport = 11/12, so 1/12 is left for refreshments: 2405/12 = £200.4167, which rounds to £200.

Data interpretation

Table 2.1

1. D – 52,600
   Can clearly be seen from table.
2. B – 1990
   Can clearly be seen from table.
3. D – Children
   4.5 New Commonwealth + 3.1 Rest of the World = 7.6 (thousand).
4. C – 200
   3.9 (thousand) in 2000 – 3.7 (thousand) in 1985 = 0.2 (thousand) = 200.
5. B – 40%
   16/40 = 40%.

Table 2.2

6. B – 50 minutes
   The ferry leaves Pier Head on the hour and returns 50 minutes later.
7. B – 1.40 pm
   Can clearly be seen from table.
8. E – 25 minutes
   Between 3.50 pm and 4.15 pm.
9. D – £110.00
   50 x £2.20 = £110.00.
10. E – 7.15 pm
    A 15 minute delay on the last four journeys would result in an hour's delay overall, so the finish time is 6.15 pm + 1 hour = 7.15 pm.

Table 2.3

11. D – 4
    Can clearly be seen from table.
12. B – x2
    Can easily be calculated from table.

13. D – 150°F
     475 less 325.
14. C – 210°C
     200°C * 105% = 210°C.

Figure 2.1
15. A – £0.99
     Can clearly be seen from table: PURE ORANGE
     JUICEX1LTR.
16. D – £3.78
     2 multisave items: £1.79 + £1.99 = £3.78.
17. E – £6.48
     Although the total items indicated by 'g' add up to £8.27,
     there is a multisave of £1.79 on S SATSUMA LARGE; thus
     £8.27 – £1.79 = £6.48.
18. C – £30.26
     £302.60 * 10% = £30.26.

Table 2.4
19. C
     23 days entitlement –1 taken last year – 11 taken in the
     current year = 11.
20. D
     Hasan receives 26 days, which equals a basic 23 days for
     the first two years' service plus 3 more days. This is 1 day
     per year (half a day per half year) so he has been with the
     company for 3 plus 2 years = 5 years in total.
21. C
     23 days annual entitlement – 1.5 days taken last year – 8
     days taken in the current year = 13.5 days. £300 / 5 = £60
     x 13.5 = £810
22. E – 4
     S Brown has 23 less 12 days' holiday left (1 taken last year,
     11 taken in the current year), equals11 days. If he takes
     these 11, he needs 4 more days of unpaid leave.

Table 2.5

23. C

     31(units sold) x £49 (price per package) = £1,519 sales income. 3% commission = £45.57.

24. A

     24 + 31 + 28 + 21 + 26 + 26 = 156 / 6= 26.

25. E

     The commission for the first 25 units is calculated at 3% and equals £36.75. The commission for the three units achieved over the target is calculated at 5% and equals £7.35. This gives a total of £44.10.

26. E

     Four out of six employees reached the target.

Table 2.6

27. C – E

     The most profitable product is identified by subtracting the total cost from sales price.

28. D

     Reducing the manufacturing cost of £2 by 50% will add £1 to the sales revenue for each unit sold. So the sales revenue is the existing £37,625 plus £21,500 = £59,125.

29. B

     £7.99 – £5.37 = £2.62 (revenue per unit) x 11,750 (number of units) = £30,785.00

30. A

     23% of £743,578.00 = £171,022.94 tax paid. £743,578.00 – £171,022.94 = £572,555.06 net profit.

Table 2.7

31. A

     (0 + 10 + 21.5 + 4)/4 = 8.9 approx.

32. B

     3.5 – (–1) = 4.5°C

33. C

34. F

     Cumulative temperature in 2000: (1.5 + 15.5 + 23 + 2) = 42. Final quarter 2001 is 42 – 2 – 14.5 – 25= 0.5.

Word swap

1. movement / tone
2. work / result
3. artificial / natural
4. some/ and
5. remain / recess
6. most / each
7. to / is
8. style / hunger
9. over / now
10. by / of
11. eat / respect
12. kill / catch
13. rake / forget
14. numerous / bitter
15. adaptable / Roman
16. inserted / impervious
17. idyllic / irritating
18. known / health
19. about / without

Missing words

1. effect effect
2. dependent dependant
3. accepted licence
4. conscience conscious
5. threw rear
6. hew hue
7. principle principal
8. courtesy curtsy
9. dispensary disciplinary
10. hoard horde
11. flowers flour
12. piece pierce
13. inform infirm

14. practice practise
15. stationary stationery
16. receipt recipe
17. exercises immediately
18. minor operate
19. boys boys'
20. it's its
21. plumb straight

Correct sentence

1. a) If you're looking for an evening out this month, there are big offers on musicals and pop concerts.
2. b) The consumer is protected from exploitation by a given seller by the existence of other sellers from whom he can buy.
3. c) All mammals produce eggs within which their young develop.
4. a) There are maps and travel books available for most of England's towns and cities.
5. c) Further information will be given to you when you visit the head office.
6. a) She married again, which surprised everybody who knew her.
7. b) There is a wide selection of gifts available, all of which can be ordered by post or online.
8. a) At that moment, I wished I had gone to the same university as John.
9. c) When I go to university I will have no time for reading novels.
10. b) The coach was expecting great things of the team this season.
11. a) Whenever a new book comes out they are the first to buy a copy.
12. b) There is the promise of a more secure future for those who save on a regular basis.

13. c) If the customer should return the goods, you must ensure you check them before giving a refund.
14. b) There are places where that kind of behaviour is unacceptable.
15. a) This borough is very good about providing bins for recycling metal, plastic, glass and paper.
16. c) One of the most important notes on the piano is Middle C.
17. b) Once Simon gets angry it takes a long while for him to calm down.
18. a) We pitched our tent on the bank of the river Stour, near where it joins the Avon.
19. c) They were walking along the beach all day yesterday and they will be walking along the cliff all day tomorrow.
20. a) It was Galileo who discovered that Jupiter has moons.

Answers and explanations to Chapter 3

Mock test 1

Quantitative reasoning

1. F
   $(7 \times 27) + (4 \times 19) = 265p = £2.65$.
2. D
   $14.45 + 27 m = 15.12$
3. F
   End of year 1: $1,000.00 \times 105\% = £1,050.00$. End of year 2: $1,050.00 \times 105\% = £1,102.50$. End of year 3: $1,102.50 \times 105\% = £1,157.63$.
4. C
   End of year 1: $800 - 40\% = £480$. End of year 2: $480 - 25\% = £360$. End of year 3: $360 - 25\% = £270$.
5. F
   30 wpm x 30 min = 900 words.
6. E
   $1.25 \times 4 = 5$.

7. D

    $(2 \times 1.75) + (5 \times 1.15) = 9.25 \times 1.175\% = £10.87.$

8. B

    $18,900 / 9 = 2,100.\ 2,100 \times 3 = 6,300.$

9. D

    $1\ kg / 5 = 200\ gm.\ £3.50 / 5 = £0.70.$

10. A

    The return journey takes 1.5 h. The meeting takes another 1.5 h. The total time spent away from the office is 3 h.

11. D

12. C

    The price of two items = 100%. If one item is for free 50% is saved.

13. C

    $3.4 / 4.3 = 0.79 \times 2.3 = £1.82$

14. B

    47 mph = 47/60 = 0.783 mpminute; 38 miles = 38/0.783 = 48.53 minutes.

    38 mph = 38/60 = 0.633mpminute; 29 miles = 29/0.633 = 45.81 = 46.21 minutes.

    48.53 − 46.21 = 2.32 minutes which rounds to 3 minutes.

15. F

    If £24 is 3%, then 1% is 24/3 = £8, and 100% = £800.

16. D

    The new price is £10 − 25% = £7.50. £1000 / £7.50 = 133.33. The sales should increase by 33.3%.

17. E

    The ratio of staple boxes can be expressed as 1 : 1.5 : 2.25 : 3.375, which sums to 8.125. 1000 gm / 8.13 = 123 x 3.375 = 415.125 gm.

18. C

    3.5% of 1,000 = £35. To obtain £35 commission B must sell 35/.03 goods equals £116.67 worth.

19. E

   The time difference between Dubai and New York is 10 hours. It is 10 hours earlier in Dubai so the conference will start at 04.30 am on 11 Jan 02.

20. F

   The ratio is 2:7:1 which can also be expressed as = 1:3.5:0.5.

21. D

   100/20 = 5 x 3 = 15%

22. F

   7.99 x 0.305 = £2.44

23. B

   225/0.45 = 500

24. C

   In 30 mins it will travel 17.5 miles divided by 0.621 equals 28 km approx.

25. C

   £12 / 25 = £0.48 per minute. £0.48 x 45 = £21.60.

26. E

   If 1 ft = 0.305 m, 1 sq ft = (0.305 x 0.305) sq m = 0.093 sq m. Price per sq m: £6.25/0.093 = £67.20. Price for 5 sq m = £67.20 x 5 = £336.

27. D

   35 mph + (35 / 2) = 52.5 / 2 = 26.25

28. B

   (5,000 + 1,000) x 2 = 12,000. (12,000 + 1,000) x 2 = 26,000.

29. F

   1.83 m = (1.83/0.305) = 6 ft. 12 files per ft, so 6 x 12 = 72 files can be stored.

30. B

   Distance/time 57 miles/70 min = 0.8 miles per minute. 0.8 miles per minute x 60 min = 48 mph

Mock test 2

Data interpretation

Table 3.1

1. B
    Readily seen from table.
2. D
    64 + 39 + 95 + 40 + 17 + 14 = 269.
3. D
    33/ 200 = 16.5%.
4. C
    42/300 x 100 = 14%, the lowest percentage.

Table 3.2

5. E
    280 Rd / selling price 3.18 = £88.05
6. B
    1,750.00 x 2.99– 4.5% = 4,997.03.
7. E
    4,997.03 / 2.79 = 1791.05 – 4.5% = 1,710.45
8. A
    (1.55 +1.66)/2=1.605 average rate. €0.5/1.605 = £0.31.

Table 3.3

9. D
    1 / 6 = 16.66%.
10. F
    £1 per week x 26.5 = £26.50.
11. C
    £23.45 – £20 + £800 – £95 = £708.45.
12. A
    – £250 + £360 – £25 = £85.

Table 3.4

13. C

 A letter to Aberdeen =£1.66 + £0.85 = £2.51. A letter to France = £0.37.

14. A

 0.96 kg = 960gm = 500gm + 460gm. 500 (£1.66) + 250 (£0.85) + 210 (£0.85) = £3.36.

15. F

 100 gm to Europe = £0.99 + 350 gm to UK = £1.30 = £2.29.

16. E

 Separately: £1.05 + £1.79 = £2.84. Together: £2.16 + £1.25 = £3.41. Difference: £0.57.

Table 3.5

17. B

 If there were 9.2 deaths per 1000, than there were 9,200 deaths per million. Since there are 83 million people in Germany = 9,200 x 83 = 763,600.

18. B

 Total births – total deaths = 3 per thousand = 3,000 deaths per million. = 3,000 x 60 = 180,000.

19. C

 End of 2001 = 60,180,000 total population. End of 2002 = 60,180,000 x 100.3% = 60,360,540.

20. E

 Total births – total deaths per year.

Table 3.6

21. F

 Arable land, permanent pasture and woodland; 33%
 Therefore 67% of land = 545,630 x 67% = 365,572 sq km.

22. C

 1km = 0.625 miles. 1 sq km = 0.39 sq m. 41,526 x 0.39 = 16,195.14.

23. F
     7643 / 41526 = 18.4%.
24. F
     30% of 504,732.

Mock test 3

Verbal reasoning
1. half / take
2. pans / knives
3. name / guest
4. actual / written
5. fact / that
6. traffic / winds
7. spiders / people
8. problems / aspects
9. benefit / communicate
10. essential / current
11. rung / fixed
12. guests aisle
13. sergeant required
14. transferred regiment
15. honorary president
16. pare excess
17. reign seemed
18. quay board
19. cheque because
20. eat ate

Mock test 4

Correct sentence
1. b) If she had only listened to me, this would never have happened.
2. c) There are just three things you need to know about Jack.
3. b) If I were you I'd see a doctor.

4.   a) It looks like everyone has gone to the cinema.

5.   b) Either Jane or her sister is bringing the dessert.

6.   c) If I hadn't had my seatbelt on I would be dead.

7.   b) From Thursday you cannot have either the blue or the black pens.

8.   a) I have been informed that neither Mandy nor Helen will be able to be there on Saturday.

9.   b) Owning a dog is very different from owning a cat.

10. a) Compared with analogue TV, digital TV provides the consumer with a greater choice of programmes to watch.

11. c) If you were to go fishing at night you might find that you catch more fish than during the day.

12. a) Although the house and barn are on the same property, they will be sold separately.

13. b) The school has insisted that no child leaves the playground until their parent arrives.

14. b) The Managing Director wanted you and me to attend the meeting.

15. b) Each night before I go to bed I make myself a cup of cocoa.

16. a) Carol thought it an honour to receive an MBE.

17. c) It looks as if it is going to rain.

18. b) Every one of the new computers in the main office has been virus checked.

19. a) It is equally important to check your credit card statement as it is your bank statement.

20. c) Mike always seems to do it that way.

Answers and explanations to Chapter 4

Verbal test

	1st	2nd	3rd	4th
1.	D	A	C	B
2.	C	D	B	A
3.	B	D	A	C
4.	D	C	B	A
5.	C	B	D	A
6.	B	D	C	A
7.	C	B	A	D
8.	D	C	A	B
9.	C	B	D	A
10.	B	D	C	A
11.	C	A	D	B
12.	B	A	D	C
13.	A	D	C	B
14.	B	A	D	C
15.	C	B	A	D
16.	D	B	C	A
17.	C	D	B	A
18.	B	A	D	C
19.	C	A	D	B
20.	D	B	C	A
21.	C	A	B	D
22.	A	B	C	D
23.	D	A	B	C
24.	C	B	D	A
25.	B	C	D	A
26.	D	A	C	B
27.	C	A	D	B
28.	B	D	A	C
29.	D	B	C	A
30.	C	B	D	A
31.	D	C	B	A
32.	B	A	D	C
33.	C	A	D	B

Quantitative reasoning test

Core equation for this set of questions: $C = 2A + B$

1

A	B	C
9	4	22
4	2	10
11	7	29
18	2	38
3	?	19

0	0	0
1	1	1
2	2	2
3	3	3
4	4	4
5	5	5
6	6	6
7	7	7
8	8	8
9	9	9

Explanation
In this question, the relationship between each row is: $B = C - 2A$. Therefore if you take the value of A (3) and multiply it by 2 and then subtract this result (6) from C (19), you obtain the value of B which is $19 - 6 = 13$.

2

A	B	C
4	17	25
12	2	26
3	3	9
14	4	32
17	1	?

0	0	0
1	1	1
2	2	2
3	3	3
4	4	4
5	5	5
6	6	6
7	7	7
8	8	8
9	9	9

Explanation
In this question, the relationship between each row is: $C = 2A + B$. Therefore if you take the value of A (17), multiply it by 2, then add this result (34) to B (1) you obtain the value of C which is $34 + 1 = 35$.

3

A	B	C
5	2	12
3	12	18
5	4	14
7	5	19
?	7	19

0	0	0
1	1	1
2	2	2
3	3	3
4	4	4
5	5	5
6	6	6
7	7	7
8	8	8
9	9	9

Explanation
In this question, the relationship between each row is: A = (C – B) / 2. Therefore if you take the value of B (7) and subtract it from C (19) and then divide this result (12) by 2 you obtain the value of A which is (19 – 7) / 2 = 6.

Core equation for this set of questions: C = 3B + A

4

A	B	C
4	1	7
8	4	20
2	3	11
4	3	13
11	32	?

0	0	0
1	1	1
2	2	2
3	3	3
4	4	4
5	5	5
6	6	6
7	7	7
8	8	8
9	9	9

Explanation
In this question, the relationship between each row is: C = 3B + A. Therefore if you take the value of B (32), multiply it by 3 and add this result (96) to A (11) you obtain the value of C which is (3 x 32) + 11 = 107.

5

A	B	C
4	15	49
12	9	39
175	19	232
25	14	67
3	?	18

0	0	0
1	1	1
2	2	2
3	3	3
4	4	4
5	5	5
6	6	6
7	7	7
8	8	8
9	9	9

Explanation
In this question, the relationship between each row is: $B = (C - A) / 3$. Therefore if you take the value of A (3) and subtract it from C (18) and then divide this result (15) by 3 you obtain the value of B which is $(18 - 3) / 3 = 5$.

6

A	B	C
17	2	23
12	3	21
15	5	30
14	2	20
?	3	28

0	0	0
1	1	1
2	2	2
3	3	3
4	4	4
5	5	5
6	6	6
7	7	7
8	8	8
9	9	9

Explanation
In this question, the relationship between each row is: $A = C - 3B$. Therefore if you take the value of B (3), multiply it by 3, then subtract this result (9) from C (28), you obtain the value of A which is $28 - (3 \times 3) = 19$.

Core equation for this set of questions: $C = 2A - (B + 1)$

7

A	B	C
4	3	4
3	6	−1
14	3	24
1	2	−1
12	6	?

0	0	0
1	1	1
2	2	2
3	3	3
4	4	4
5	5	5
6	6	6
7	7	7
8	8	8
9	9	9

Explanation
In this question, the relationship between each row is: $C = 2A - (B + 1)$. Therefore if you add 1 to the value of B (6) and subtract this result (7) from A (12) multiplied by 2, you obtain the value of C which is $(2 \times 12) - (6 + 1) = 17$.

8

A	B	C
12	1	22
34	13	54
3	0	5
15	12	17
21	14	?

0	0	0
1	1	1
2	2	2
3	3	3
4	4	4
5	5	5
6	6	6
7	7	7
8	8	8
9	9	9

Explanation
In this question, the relationship between each row is: $C = 2A - (B + 1)$. Therefore if you add 1 to the value of B (14) and subtract this result (15) from A (21) multiplied by 2 you obtain the value of C which is $(2 \times 21) - (14 + 1) = 27$.

9

A	B	C
14	13	14
21	2	39
3	2	3
2	1	2
5	9	?

0	0	0
1	1	1
2	2	2
3	3	3
4	4	4
5	5	5
6	6	6
7	7	7
8	8	8
9	9	9

Explanation
In this question, the relationship between each row is: $C = 2A - (B + 1)$. Therefore if you add 1 to the value of B (9) and subtract this result (10) from A (5) multiplied by 2 you obtain the value of C which is $(2 \times 5) - (9 + 1) = 0$.

Core equation for this set of questions: $C = 6A - 2B$

10

A	B	C
7	26	−10
3	14	−10
2	6	0
5	20	−10
13	38	?

0	0	0
1	1	1
2	2	2
3	3	3
4	4	4
5	5	5
6	6	6
7	7	7
8	8	8
9	9	9

Explanation
In this question, the relationship between each row is: $C = 6A - 2B$. Therefore if you take the value of A (13), multiply it by 6 then subtract B (38) multiplied by 2 you obtain the value of C which is $(6 \times 13) - (2 \times 38) = 2$.

11

A	B	C
6	12	12
2	2	8
15	66	−42
68	344	−280
123	16	?

0	0	0
1	1	1
2	2	2
3	3	3
4	4	4
5	5	5
6	6	6
7	7	7
8	8	8
9	9	9

Explanation
In this question, the relationship between each row is: C = 6A – 2B. Therefore if you take the value of A (123), multiply it by 6, then subtract B (16) multiplied by 2, you obtain the value of C which is (6 x 123) – (2 x 16) = 706.

12

A	B	C
1	1	4
24	60	24
2	−5	22
6	8	20
11	25	?

0	0	0
1	1	1
2	2	2
3	3	3
4	4	4
5	5	5
6	6	6
7	7	7
8	8	8
9	9	9

Explanation
In this question, the relationship between each row is: C = 6A – 2B. Therefore if you take the value of A (11) and multiply it by 6 and then subtract B (25) multiplied by 2 you obtain the value of C which is (6 x 11) – (2 x 25) = 16.

Core equation for this set of questions: A + B + C = 180

13

A	B	C
35	60	85
25	65	90
10	10	160
24	48	108
50	22	?

0	*0*	0
1	1	1
2	2	2
3	3	3
4	4	4
5	5	5
6	6	6
7	7	7
8	8	*8*
9	9	9

Explanation
In this question, the relationship between each row is: A + B + C = 180. Therefore if you take the value of A (55), add it to the value of B (22) and subtract this number (77) from 180, you obtain the value of C which is $180 - (50 + 22) = 108$.

14

A	B	C
37	27	116
88	0	92
120	19	41
25	92	63
?	0	172

0	*0*	0
1	1	1
2	2	2
3	3	3
4	4	4
5	5	5
6	6	6
7	7	7
8	8	*8*
9	9	9

Explanation
In this question, the relationship between each row is: A + B + C = 180. Therefore if you take the value of B (0) add it to the value of C (172) and subtract this number from 180 you obtain the value of A which is $180 - (172) = 8$.

15

A	B	C
17	77	86
12	32	136
15	80	85
14	14	152
25	?	83

0	0	0
1	1	1
2	2	2
3	3	3
4	4	4
5	5	5
6	6	6
7	7	7
8	8	8
9	9	9

Explanation

In this question, the relationship between each row is: A + B + C = 180. Therefore if you take the value of A (25) add it to the value of C (83) and subtract this number (108) from 180 you obtain the value of A which is 180 – (108) = 72.

Core equation for this set of questions: C = A – B

16

A	B	C
822	144	678
728	214	514
373	212	161
882	215	667
877	678	?

0	0	0
1	1	1
2	2	2
3	3	3
4	4	4
5	5	5
6	6	6
7	7	7
8	8	8
9	9	9

Explanation

In this question, the relationship between each row is: C = A – B. Therefore if you take the value of A (877) and subtract the value of B (678) from it you obtain the value of C which is 877 – 678 = 199.

17

A	B	C
8.4	7.2	1.2
17.8	14.7	3.1
27.3	13.2	14.1
92.4	77.1	15.3
78.3	43.2	?

0	0	0.0
1	1	0.1
2	2	0.2
3	3	0.3
4	4	0.4
5	5	0.5
6	6	0.6
7	7	0.7
8	8	0.8
9	9	0.9

Note: in these questions the columns correspond to 10s, 1s and 0.1s.

Explanation
In this question, the relationship between each row is: C = A – B. Therefore if you take the value of A (78.3) and subtract the value of B (43.2) from it you obtain the value of C which is 78.3 – 43.2 = 35.1.

18

A	B	C
71	12	59
82	11	71
93	10	83
104	9	95
115	8	?

0	0	0
1	1	1
2	2	2
3	3	3
4	4	4
5	5	5
6	6	6
7	7	7
8	8	8
9	9	9

Explanation
In this question, the relationship between each row is: C = A – B. Therefore if you take the value of A (115) and subtract the value of B (8) from it you obtain the value of C which is 115 – 8 = 107.

Core equation for this set of questions: $C = A^2$

19

A	B	C
3.3	0	10.89
7.3	0	53.29
13	0	169
19	0	361
20	0	?

0	0	0
1	1	1
2	2	2
3	3	3
4	4	4
5	5	5
6	6	6
7	7	7
8	8	8
9	9	9

Explanation
In this question, the relationship between each row is: $C = A^2$. Therefore if you take the value of A (20) and multiply it by itself you obtain the value of C which is (20 x 20) = 400. The numbers in column B are unused, but you should still recognize the pattern of squares in column C.

20

A	B	C
3	12	9
4	32	16
5	14	25
6	12	36
7	8	?

0	0	0
1	1	1
2	2	2
3	3	3
4	4	4
5	5	5
6	6	6
7	7	7
8	8	8
9	9	9

Explanation
In this question, the relationship between each row is: $C = A^2$. Therefore if you take the value of A (7) and multiply it by itself you obtain the value of C which is (7 x 7) = 49.

The numbers in column B are unused, but you should still recognize the pattern of squares in column C.

21

A	B	C
5	400	25
10	395	100
15	390	225
20	385	400
25	380	?

0	0	0
1	1	1
2	2	2
3	3	3
4	4	4
5	5	5
6	6	6
7	7	7
8	8	8
9	9	9

Explanation

In this question, the relationship between each row is: $C = A^2$. Therefore if you take the value of A (25) and multiply it by itself you obtain the value of C which is (25 x 25) = 625. The numbers in column B are unused, but you should still recognize the pattern of squares in column C.

Core equation for this set of questions: $C = 3A - B$

22

A	B	C
4	1	11
16	44	4
72	25	191
26	26	52
50	25	?

0	0	0
1	1	1
2	2	2
3	3	3
4	4	4
5	5	5
6	6	6
7	7	7
8	8	8
9	9	9

Explanation

In this question, the relationship between each row is: $C = 3A - B$. Therefore if you take the value of A (50), multiply it by 3 then subtract B (25) from this result (150), you obtain the value of C which is (3 x 50) – 25 = 125.

23

A	B	C
14	15	27
12	9	27
5	5	10
4	5	7
3	5	?

0	0	0
1	1	1
2	2	2
3	3	3
4	4	4
5	5	5
6	6	6
7	7	7
8	8	8
9	9	9

Explanation

In this question, the relationship between each row is: C = 3A − B. Therefore if you take the value of A (3), multiply it by 3 then subtract B (5) from this result (9), you obtain the value of C which is (3 x 3) − 5 = 4.

24

A	B	C
17	2	49
12	3	33
15	5	40
14	2	40
13	13	?

0	0	0
1	1	1
2	2	2
3	3	3
4	4	4
5	5	5
6	6	6
7	7	7
8	8	8
9	9	9

Explanation

In this question, the relationship between each row is: C = 3A − B. Therefore if you take the value of A (13), multiply it by 3 then subtract B (13) from this result (39), you obtain the value of C which is (3 x 13) − 13 = 26.

Core equation for this set of questions: C = AB – 1

25

A	B	C
5	3	14
17	3	50
2	3	5
4	3	11
11	3	?

0	0	0
1	1	1
2	2	2
3	3	3
4	4	4
5	5	5
6	6	6
7	7	7
8	8	8
9	9	9

Explanation
In this question, the relationship between each row is: C = AB – 1. Therefore if you multiply A(11) by B (3) and subtract 1 from this result (33) you obtain the value of C which is (3 x 11) – 1 = 32.

Harder questions

Core equation for this set of questions: $C = (\sqrt{A}) + \sqrt{B}$

1

A	B	C
9	4	5
625	400	45
1600	900	70
100	4	12
225	25	?

0	0	0
1	1	1
2	2	2
3	3	3
4	4	4
5	5	5
6	6	6
7	7	7
8	8	8
9	9	9

Explanation

In this question, the relationship between each row is: $C = \sqrt{A} + \sqrt{B}$. Therefore if you take the square root of A (225) and add the square root of B (25) to this result you obtain the value of C which is $\sqrt{225} + \sqrt{25} = 20$.

2

A	B	C
49	4	9
64	9	11
81	16	13
100	36	16
144	64	?

0	0	0
1	1	1
2	2	2
3	3	3
4	4	4
5	5	5
6	6	6
7	7	7
8	8	8
9	9	9

Explanation

In this question, the relationship between each row is: $C = (\sqrt{A}) + (\sqrt{B})$. Therefore if you take the square root of A (144) and add the square root of B (64) to the result you obtain the value of C which is $\sqrt{144} + \sqrt{64} = 20$.

3

A	B	C
576	4	26
529	16	27
484	64	30
441	121	32
400	100	?

0	0	0
1	1	1
2	2	2
3	3	3
4	4	4
5	5	5
6	6	6
7	7	7
8	8	8
9	9	9

Explanation
In this question, the relationship between each row is: $C = (\sqrt{A} + \sqrt{B})$. Therefore if you take the square root of A (400) and add the square root of B (100) to the result you obtain the value of C which is $\sqrt{400} + \sqrt{100} = 30$.

Core equation for this set of questions: $C = (3 \times B^2) - A$

4

A	B	C
12	4	36
18	4	30
14	5	61
29	6	79
15	5	?

0	0	0
1	1	1
2	2	2
3	3	3
4	4	4
5	5	5
6	6	6
7	7	7
8	8	8
9	9	9

Explanation
In this question, the relationship between each row is: $C = (3 \times B^2) - A$. Therefore if you square the value of B (5), multiply the result (25) by 3 and subtract A (15) from this number (75), you obtain the value of C which is $(3 \times 25) - 15 = 60$.

5

A	B	C		0	0	0
				1	1	1
100	9	143		2	2	2
				3	3	3
200	14	388		4	4	4
				5	5	5
300	12	132		6	6	6
				7	7	7
400	15	275		8	8	8
				9	9	9
200	12	?				

Explanation

In this question, the relationship between each row is: C = (3 x B²) – A. Therefore if you square the value of B (12), multiply the result (144) by 3 and subtract A (200) from this number (432), you obtain the value of C which is (3 x 144) – 200 = 232.

6

A	B	C		0	0	0
				1	1	1
200	20	1000		2	2	2
				3	3	3
150	22	1302		4	4	4
				5	5	5
12	4	36		6	6	6
				7	7	7
488	14	100		8	8	8
				9	9	9
250	20	?				

Explanation

In this question, the relationship between each row is: C = (3 x B²) – A. Therefore if you square the value of B (20), multiply the result (400) by 3 and subtract A (250) from this number (1200), you obtain the value of C which is (3 x 400) – 250 = 950.

Core equation for this set of questions: $C = 2A \times 2B$

7

A	B	C
2	3	24
5	12	240
13	3	156
6	10	240
12	2	?

0	0	0
1	1	1
2	2	2
3	3	3
4	4	4
5	5	5
6	6	6
7	7	7
8	8	8
9	9	9

Explanation
In this question, the relationship between each row is: $C = 2A \times 2B$. Therefore if you take 2 times the value of B (2) and multiply it by 2 times the value of A (12) you obtain the value of C which is $4 \times 24 = 96$.

8

A	B	C
4	6	96
4	7	112
4	5	80
4	4	64
4	8	?

0	0	0
1	1	1
2	2	2
3	3	3
4	4	4
5	5	5
6	6	6
7	7	7
8	8	8
9	9	9

Explanation
In this question, the relationship between each row is: $C = 2A \times 2B$. Therefore if you take 2 times the value of B (8) and multiply it by 2 times the value of A (4), you obtain the value of C which is $16 \times 8 = 128$.

9

A	B	C
12	5	240
5	4	80
6	8	192
5	12	240
10	5	?

0	0	0
1	1	1
2	2	2
3	3	3
4	4	4
5	5	5
6	6	6
7	7	7
8	8	8
9	9	9

Explanation
In this question, the relationship between each row is: C = 2A x 2B. Therefore if you take 2 times the value of B (5) and multiply it by 2 times the value of A (10), you obtain the value of C which is 20 x 10 = 200.

Core equation for this set of questions: $C = \sqrt{B} - \sqrt{A}$

10

A	B	C
16	64	4
144	225	3
1	16	3
4	16	2
16	256	?

0	0	0
1	1	1
2	2	2
3	3	3
4	4	4
5	5	5
6	6	6
7	7	7
8	8	8
9	9	9

Explanation
In this question, the relationship between each row is: $C = \sqrt{B} - \sqrt{A}$. Therefore if you take the square root of B (256) and subtract the square root of A (16) from the result you obtain the value of C, which is 16 – 4 = 12.

11

A	B	C
256	1024	16
25	900	25
16	256	12
64	256	8
1600	2500	?

0	0	0
1	1	1
2	2	2
3	3	3
4	4	4
5	5	5
6	6	6
7	7	7
8	8	8
9	9	9

Explanation
In this question, the relationship between each row is: $C = \sqrt{B} - \sqrt{A}$. Therefore if you take the square root of B (2500) and subtract the square root of A (1600) from the result you obtain the value of C, which is $50 - 40 = 10$.

12

A	B	C
1225	2025	10
625	2025	20
625	625	0
49	2025	38
9	169	?

0	0	0
1	1	1
2	2	2
3	3	3
4	4	4
5	5	5
6	6	6
7	7	7
8	8	8
9	9	9

Explanation
In this question, the relationship between each row is: $C = \sqrt{B} - \sqrt{A}$. Therefore if you take the square root of B (169) and subtract the square root of A (9) from the result, you obtain the value of C, which is $13 - 3 = 10$.

Core equation for this set of questions: C = 360 − (A + B)

13

A	B	C
124	42	194
80	45	235
22	148	190
35	170	155
50	145	?

0	0	0
1	1	1
2	2	2
3	3	3
4	4	4
5	5	5
6	6	6
7	7	7
8	8	8
9	9	9

Explanation
In this question, the relationship between each row is: C = 360 − (A + B). Therefore if you take the value of A (50) + B (145) and subtract this number (195) from 360 you obtain the value of C, which is 360 − 195 = 165.

14

A	B	C
200	67	93
45	98	217
76	22	262
40	195	125
104	256	?

0	0	0
1	1	1
2	2	2
3	3	3
4	4	4
5	5	5
6	6	6
7	7	7
8	8	8
9	9	9

Explanation
In this question, the relationship between each row is: C = 360 − (A + B). Therefore if you take the value of A (104) + B (256) and subtract this number (360) from 360 you obtain the value of C which is 360 − 360 = 0.

15

A	B	C
10	20	330
40	30	290
70	40	250
150	50	160
220	60	?

0	0	0
1	1	1
2	2	2
3	3	3
4	4	4
5	5	5
6	6	6
7	7	7
8	8	8
9	9	9

Explanation
In this question, the relationship between each row is: C = 360 − (A + B). Therefore if you take the value of A (220) + B (60) and subtract this number (280) from 360 you obtain the value of C, which is 360 −280 = 80.

Core equation for this set of questions: C = (A x B) – B

16

A	B	C
4	4	12
10	5	45
1	5	0
5	1	4
5	10	?

0	0	0
1	1	1
2	2	2
3	3	3
4	4	4
5	5	5
6	6	6
7	7	7
8	8	8
9	9	9

Explanation
In this question, the relationship between each row is: C = (A x B) – B. Therefore if you take the value of A (5) multiplied by B (10) and subtract the value of B (10) from the result (50) you obtain the value of C, which is (5 x 10) – 10 = 40.

Data interpretation test

Figure 4.1

1. A – 44
   Brian will not be 45 until his birthday the next day.
2. D – 30 years
   The difference between 1985 and 1955, both being born on the same day
3. D – January 1964
   The only time when Brian and James were both aged 4 years is between 17.01.1964 (James's 4th birthday) and 01.02.1964 (the eve of Brian's 5th birthday).
4. B – £5.00
   If the difference is equal to 25%, then £15.00 must be 75%. Therefore £15.00/3 = 25% = £5.00.

Table 4.1

5. E – Air, commodity & ship brokers
   They have the lowest percentage increase at 22.0%.
6. E – £19,164.50
   For 2002: total earnings = £1,000,685, average earnings = £1,000,685/20 = £50,034.25. For 1991: total earnings = £617,395, average earnings = £617,395/20 = £30,869.75. Therefore 2001 average – 1991 average = £50,034.25 – £30,869.75 = £ 19,164.50.
7. D – 301.6%
   To be ranked first, air traffic planners & controllers must earn at least £110,342 in 2001 (£1 more than general managers). This would be an increase from their 1991 earnings of (£110,342 – £27,476) / £27,476 * 100 = 301.6%.
8. C – 8th
   An increase of 166.3% would produce a salary of £47,007, placing professional athletes above industrial underwriters and claims assessors, but below doctors.

Table 4.2

9. C – 1989–90
    Growth in earnings increased by £11.40 between 1989 and 1990, higher than any other year.
10. E – £125.80
    £353.40 – £227.60 = £125.80.
11. A – 36.1%
    £353.40 – £259.70 = £93.70 / £259.70 * 100 = 36.1%.
12. B – £80.23
    Average non-manual men's wages (£285.46) – average manual men's wages (£205.23) = £80.23.

Table 4.3

13. C – £4,727
    Addition of the 1991 figures for Higher, Further and Adult Education (£3,734 million) + Polytechnics and Colleges Funding Council (£993 million) = £4,727 million.
14. F – 50.0%
    8287 – 5523 = 2764 / 5523 * 100 = 50.0%.
15. E – £667,471 million
    Total expenditure (£34,041 million) = 5.1% of GDP. Therefore (£34,041/5.1) * 100 = £667,471 million.
16. B – 11.0%
    VAT amount (£2,705)/Sub-total of expenditure before VAT (£21,913 + £2, 678) = £24,591 = 11.0%.

Analysis of information test

Type A questions

Passage 1

1. True
    The blue line is described as running north–south and the red line runs east–west so the angle at the point of intersection must be 90 degrees.

2.   True
      It is clear from the text that the blue line runs north–south
      and the red line east–west. It is also said that the green line
      intersects the red line east of the blue line and the grey line
      intersects the blue line south of the red line. This means
      that the grey line would intersect the red line west of the
      green line.

3.   False
      As the blue line runs north–south the intersections of the
      yellow and green line with the blue line will take place at
      the same east–west position.

4.   Impossible to say
      There is no information contained within the text to
      indicate the starting or end positions of the lines.

Passage 2

5.   False
      It is clear from the text that the eurozone rate is expected
      to remain unchanged.

6.   True
      It is stated that the Yen's recent strength is not sustainable.

7.   Impossible to say
      It is unclear from the passage whether or not the two
      currencies are currently aligned or will continue to be.

Passage 3

8.   True
      As Team 4 has won more games that Team 1 and has not
      lost any games, Team 4 must have more points than Team
      1 as they have played the same number of games.

9.   False
      Team 3 has seven more points than Team 2 and Team 6
      has four more points than Team 2. This means that Team 3
      has three more points than Team 6.

10. Impossible to say
     Although it can be proved from the passage that Team 2
     will have fewer points than any other of the teams listed,
     we do not know how many teams there are in the league.
     This means that it is possible there are other teams in the
     league and that they may have fewer points than Team 2.

Passage 4

11. Impossible to say
     The passage makes no comment on this issue.
12. True
     This can clearly be seen to be the case from the passage.
13. False
     The principal point concerns the enhancement of a
     manager's decisions by the incorporation of tests in the
     overall decision-making process.

Passage 5

14. True
     This answer is clearly correct from the passage.
15. True
     Because it rains consecutively on a Friday/Saturday there
     are only three days which follow rain, but on which it does
     not rain. We also know that two of these days must be
     Sundays. As there are two occasions on which the sky is
     clear all day after the rain, at least one of these must be a
     Sunday.
16. Impossible to say
     This is only true if it rains on the first Wednesday and the
     first Friday. As the passage does not identify which days it
     rains on each week, we cannot confirm that this is true.

Passage 6

17. False
     You also need to meet the earnings requirement.
18. True
     17.5% of £30,000 = £5,250.

19. True
   The passage states that all contributions qualify for tax
   relief at the highest rate paid by the saver.

Passage 7

20. True
   It is stated that the bedrooms are on the second floor and
   the kitchen family room is on the third.
21. Impossible to say
   The size of the reception room is not given.
22. True
   While the text does not state on which floor the reception
   room is on, it can be deduced that it is on the first because
   it is the only floor not described.

Passage 8

23. False
   A keyboard can be used to input to a command interface
   but it is not a command interface.
24. True
   It is clear from the text that application software is user-
   related programs.
25. True
   The passage states that the user interface is such a means
   of communication and is also described as the human
   computer interface.

Passage 9

26. True
   The passage clearly states that the velocity and
   displacement of straight line motion can be attributed
   negative values.
27. Impossible to say
   The rules of dynamics are not covered in the passage.

28. False

    The statement is true with respect to the forces that act on the particle but is false because the passage makes clear that the discipline is not limited to the study of particle motion in straight lines.

Passage 10

29. True

    Australia is in the southern hemisphere so depressions would generate winds in the counter direction to the clockwise winds of a northern hemisphere depression.

30. True

    The passage states that winds in depressions are revolving. As a depression passes the town therefore it would experience winds in opposite directions on either side of the depression. This would be the experience in either hemisphere.

31. False

    In the northern hemisphere it would be your left ear; in the southern hemisphere it would be your right.

Passage 11

32. False

    The insurance broker is on the same side of the road as the off-licence while the pharmacist is on the same side as the newsagent. It is clear, therefore, that they are not on the same side of the road as the newsagent is described as directly opposite the off-licence.

33. True

    The bus stop is across the road from the optician which in turn is across the road from the pharmacist. This means that the bus stop and the pharmacist are on the same side of the road.

34. False

    There is a two-shop gap between the post office and off licence, and this gap is in part taken up by either the clothes shop or butchers. In either event this leaves insufficient space for the optician and insurance broker. This means that the optician can not be next to the butcher.

Passage 12

35. Impossible to say

    The work would end in the right hand corner only if the worker started each line of boards in the left hand corner, but the instructions only state that the first line is started this way.

36. True

    The end board will be cut to fit the space that remains, and is likely to result in a longer or shorter leftover piece. This is to be used to start the next row so long as the difference in lengths is greater than 50 cm.

37. True

    As the board is described as having a long and short side you can deduce that the short end of the board can be called its end.

Passage 13

38. False

    The passage states that it takes Steve less time than James to get to the meeting and that it takes James 9 minutes, so the statement must be false.

39. True

    As it takes James longer to get to the meeting than Steve or Helen, and he sets off after Helen, he must arrive after she does.

40. Impossible to say

    Although Richard has to travel further we have no indication of how long his journey will take and so whether he would need to set off first in order to arrive first.

Type B questions

1. (2) , (3) , (5)

   Statement (3) tells us that the southeast line is normally twice as fast as the southwest line. Since the storm, the south-east line is running at 50% of its normal speed and the southwest line is taking an additional 30 minutes. This means that the south-east line must be faster than the southwest line by 30 minutes. Statement (2) tells us that there is a southeast line train leaving within 10 minutes of your arrival at the station, so (from 3) it must arrive in London before the first southwest train. Statement (5) tells us that the next southern line train leaves at 11:35. We already know that the southern line is the slowest, so we now know that the 11:20 southeast line train will get to London the fastest.

2. (1) and (5)

   It is a sequence of the power of 3.

3. (3) and (5)

   These statements allow Robin to establish that the bill is incorrect. Point 1 is not required as the information is already known, point 2 is not relevant as the position is permanent, point 3 is relevant as the person left the position before 12 weeks, point 4 is not required as the post was known to carry no other benefits but the salary, and point 5 is required because it explains the level at which the fee should be set.

4. (4)

   Statement (4) gives us a geographical location for the bookshop. As we know that the bookshop is two blocks north of 8 and one block east of F it must be on the junction of G and 10. With this information the bookshop can be located from any part of the city.

5. (4)

   This answer best explains the conclusion because it correctly identifies that there was discrimination and a difference of gender, but that the employer had an explanation for that differential treatment.

6.   (1) , (2)
     (1) Confirms that Simon is George's son. From (2) we can
     work out Simon's age. From these two facts, and the fact
     that George was 28 when Simon was born, we can work
     out his age.
7.   (4)
     Statements 1 and 2 are general point about maximum fee
     levels so are not relevant, statements 3–5 give specific
     information according to salary level, and statement 4
     covers the relevant band.
8.   (4)
     This question is a lot easier than it may seem. To discover
     the answer to such questions, it helps if your focus on
     words such as 'is,' 'and', 'not' and 'or' and ignore the
     subject.
9.   (1), (2), (4)
     Assets and cash are assets and debtors are a liability. The
     remaining items are irrelevant to the capital ratio so can be
     ignored.
10. (4) and (5)
     It is a sequence of cubed numbers.
11. (2)
     Remember to treat the content of these questions as true
     and resist the temptation to bring your own knowledge to
     the issue. Only statement 2 contradicts the claim that a
     ship will simply be seen to become smaller as it sails away
     and so disproves the hypothesis.
12. (1), (3),(5)
     It is a sequence of prime numbers.

Answers and explanations for Chapter 5

Mock test 1: verbal test

	1st	2nd	3rd	4th
1.	C	D	A	B
2.	B	C	A	D
3.	D	C	B	A
4.	D	C	A	B
5.	A	D	C	B
6.	B	D	C	A
7.	D	A	C	B
8.	C	D	A	B
9.	C	A	D	B
10.	D	A	C	B
11.	A	B	D	C
12.	B	D	C	A
13.	C	B	A	D
14.	D	B	C	A
15.	B	D	C	A
16.	C	B	A	D

Mock test 2: quantitative reasoning, easy to medium-hard questions

Core equation for this set of questions: $C = AB - 1$

1

A	B	C
4	15	59
12	9	107
17	19	322
3	3	8
12	14	?

0	0	0
1	1	1
2	2	2
3	3	3
4	4	4
5	5	5
6	6	6
7	7	7
8	8	8
9	9	9

Explanation
In this question, the relationship between each row is: $C = AB - 1$. Therefore if you multiply A(12) by B (14) and subtract 1 from this result (168), you obtain the value of C which is (12 x 14) – 1 = 167.

2

A	B	C
12	14	167
4	19	75
19	13	246
17	12	203
12	44	?

0	0	0
1	1	1
2	2	2
3	3	3
4	4	4
5	5	5
6	6	6
7	7	7
8	8	8
9	9	9

Explanation
In this question, the relationship between each row is: $C = AB - 1$. Therefore if you multiply A(12) by B (44) and subtract 1 from this result (528), you obtain the value of C which is (12 x 44) – 1 = 527.

Core equation for this set of questions: $C = 4B - A$

3

A	B	C
12	3	0
18	14	38
10	20	70
11	13	41
52	100	?

0	0	0
1	1	1
2	2	2
3	3	3
4	4	4
5	5	5
6	6	6
7	7	7
8	8	8
9	9	9

Explanation
In this question, the relationship between each row is: $C = 4B - A$. Therefore if you take the value of B (100), multiply it by 4 and then subtract A (52) from the result (400), you obtain the value of C which is $(100 \times 4) - 52 = 348$.

4

A	B	C
72	40	88
13	23	79
54	14	2
23	23	69
10	40	?

0	0	0
1	1	1
2	2	2
3	3	3
4	4	4
5	5	5
6	6	6
7	7	7
8	8	8
9	9	9

Explanation
In this question, the relationship between each row is: $C = 4B - A$. Therefore if you take the value of B (40), multiply it by 4 and then subtract A (10) from the result (160), you obtain the value of C which is $(40 \times 4) - 10 = 150$.

5

A	B	C
42	13	10
112	112	336
14	54	202
72	72	216
39	49	?

0	0	0
1	1	1
2	2	2
3	3	3
4	4	4
5	**5**	5
6	6	6
7	7	**7**
8	8	8
9	9	9

Explanation
In this question, the relationship between each row is: $C = 4B - A$. Therefore if you take the value of B (49), multiply it by 4 then subtract A (39) from this result (196), you obtain the value of C which is $(4 \times 49) - 39 = 157$.

Core equation for this set of questions: $C = 5A + B$

6

A	B	C
3	7	22
3	9	24
2	3	13
6	12	42
4	1	?

0	0	0
1	1	**1**
2	**2**	2
3	3	3
4	4	4
5	5	5
6	6	6
7	7	7
8	8	8
9	9	9

Explanation
In this question, the relationship between each row is: $C = 5A + B$. Therefore if you take the value of A (4), multiply it by 5 and then add B (1) to the result (20), you obtain the value of C which is $(5 \times 4) + 1 = 21$.

7

A	B	C
7	3	38
9	32	77
17	81	166
22	12	122
30	10	?

0	0	0
1	1	1
2	2	2
3	3	3
4	4	4
5	5	5
6	6	6
7	7	7
8	8	8
9	9	9

Explanation
In this question, the relationship between each row is: C = 5A + B. Therefore if you take the value of A (30), multiply it by 5 then add B (10) to the result (150), you obtain the value of C which is (5 x 30) + 10 = 160.

8

A	B	C
12	4	64
44	1	221
3	3	18
7	5	40
13	13	?

0	0	0
1	1	1
2	2	2
3	3	3
4	4	4
5	5	5
6	6	6
7	7	7
8	8	8
9	9	9

Explanation
In this question, the relationship between each row is: C = 5A + B. Therefore if you take the value of A (13), multiply it by 5 then add B (13) to the result (65), you obtain the value of C which is (5 x 13) + 13 = 78.

Core equation for this set of questions: $C = B^2 + A$

9

A	B	C
12	2	16
14	3	23
2	2	6
4	4	20
5	3	?

0	0	0
1	1	1
2	2	2
3	3	3
4	4	4
5	5	5
6	6	6
7	7	7
8	8	8
9	9	9

Explanation
In this question, the relationship between each row is: $C = B^2 + A$. Therefore if you take the value of B (3), multiply it by itself, then add this result (9) to A (5), you obtain the value of C which is $(3 \times 3) + 5 = 14$.

10

A	B	C
10	12	154
10	14	206
14	16	270
14	18	338
18	20	?

0	0	0
1	1	1
2	2	2
3	3	3
4	4	4
5	5	5
6	6	6
7	7	7
8	8	8
9	9	9

Explanation
In this question, the relationship between each row is: $C = B^2 + A$. Therefore if you take the value of B (20), multiply it by itself, then add this result (400) to A (18), you obtain the value of C which is $(20 \times 20) + 18 = 418$.

11

A	B	C
90	90	8190
12	1	13
10	10	110
15	15	240
1	12	?

0	0	0
1	1	1
2	2	2
3	3	3
4	4	4
5	5	5
6	6	6
7	7	7
8	8	8
9	9	9

Explanation
In this question, the relationship between each row is: $C = B^2 + A$. Therefore if you take the value of B (12), multiply it by itself, then add this result (144) to A (1), you obtain the value of C which is $(12 \times 12) + 1 = 145$.

Core equation for this set of questions: $C = A^2 - B$

12

A	B	C
4	4	12
3	2	7
5	3	22
9	5	76
6	2	?

0	0	0
1	1	1
2	2	2
3	3	3
4	4	4
5	5	5
6	6	6
7	7	7
8	8	8
9	9	9

Explanation
In this question, the relationship between each row is: $C = A^2 - B$. Therefore if you take the value of A (6), multiply it by itself, then subtract B (2) from this result (36), you obtain the value of C which is $(6 \times 6) - 2 = 34$.

13

A	B	C
1	0.5	0.5
12	72	72
10	4.8	95.2
5	5	20
3	1.2	?

0	0	0.0
1	1	0.1
2	2	0.2
3	3	0.3
4	4	0.4
5	5	0.5
6	6	0.6
7	7	0.7
8	8	0.8
9	9	0.9

Note: in these questions the columns correspond to 10s, 1s and 0.1s.

Explanation
In this question, the relationship between each row is: $C = A^2 - B$. Therefore if you take the value of A (3), multiply it by itself, then subtract B (1.2) from this result (9), you obtain the value of C which is $(3 \times 3) - 1.2 = 7.8$.

14

A	B	C
29	14	827
25	12	613
22	100	384
18	200	124
14	150	?

0	0	0
1	1	1
2	2	2
3	3	3
4	4	4
5	5	5
6	6	6
7	7	7
8	8	8
9	9	9

Explanation
In this question, the relationship between each row is: $C = A^2 - B$. Therefore if you take the value of A (14), multiply it by itself, then subtract B (150) from this result (196), you obtain the value of C which is $(14 \times 14) - 150 = 46$.

Core equation for this set of questions: $C = A^2 + B^2$

15

A	B	C
3	2	13
4	2	20
1	1	2
3	3	18
4	4	?

0	0	0
1	1	1
2	2	2
3	3	3
4	4	4
5	5	5
6	6	6
7	7	7
8	8	8
9	9	9

Explanation
In this question, the relationship between each row is: $C = A^2 + B^2$. Therefore if you take A (4) multiplied by itself and B (4) multiplied by itself, and add these two results (16) and (16), you obtain the value of C which is $(4 \times 4) + (4 \times 4) = 32$.

16

A	B	C
16	12	400
5	5	50
12	1	145
4	4	32
9	6	?

0	0	0
1	1	1
2	2	2
3	3	3
4	4	4
5	5	5
6	6	6
7	7	7
8	8	8
9	9	9

Explanation
In this question, the relationship between each row is: $C = A^2 + B^2$. Therefore if you take A (9) multiplied by itself and B (6) multiplied by itself and add these two results (81) and (36), you obtain the value of C which is $(9 \times 9) + (6 \times 6) = 117$.

17

A	B	C
25	20	1025
10	15	325
10	10	200
15	15	450
20	10	?

0	0	0
1	1	1
2	2	2
3	3	3
4	4	4
5	5	5
6	6	6
7	7	7
8	8	8
9	9	9

Explanation
In this question, the relationship between each row is: $C = A^2 + B^2$. Therefore if you take A (20) multiplied by itself and B (10) multiplied by itself and add these two results (400) and (100), you obtain the value of C which is (20 x 20) + (10 x 10) = 500.

Core equation for this set of questions: $C = \sqrt{A} - B$

18

A	B	C
4	1	1
49	2	5
100	4	6
121	3	8
16	4	?

0	0	0
1	1	1
2	2	2
3	3	3
4	4	4
5	5	5
6	6	6
7	7	7
8	8	8
9	9	9

Explanation
In this question, the relationship between each row is: $C = \sqrt{A} - B$. Therefore if you take the square root of A (16) and subtract B (4) from the result (4), you obtain the value of C, which is 4 – 4 = 0.

19

A	B	C
196	12	2
64	0	8
121	10.1	0.9
289	12	5
10000	91.2	?

0	0	0.0
1	1	0.1
2	2	0.2
3	3	0.3
4	4	0.4
5	5	0.5
6	6	0.6
7	7	0.7
8	8	0.8
9	9	0.9

Note: in these questions the columns correspond to 10s, 1s and 0.1s.

Explanation
In this question, the relationship between each row is: $C = \sqrt{A} - B$. Therefore if you take the square root of A (10000) and subtract B (91.2) from the result (100), you obtain the value of C which is $100 - 91.2 = 8.8$.

20

A	B	C
36	4	2
64	5	3
144	10	2
625	14	11
1600	12	?

0	0	0
1	1	1
2	2	2
3	3	3
4	4	4
5	5	5
6	6	6
7	7	7
8	8	8
9	9	9

Explanation
In this question, the relationship between each row is: $C = \sqrt{A} - B$. Therefore if you take the square root of A (1600) and subtract B (12) from the result (40), you obtain the value of C which is $40 - 12 = 28$.

Mock test 3: verbal test

	1st	2nd	3rd	4th
1.	D	C	A	B
2.	D	B	A	C
3.	B	D	C	A
4.	D	B	C	A
5.	C	D	A	B
6.	C	A	D	B
7.	A	D	B	C
8.	D	B	C	A
9.	D	C	B	A
10.	B	D	A	C
11.	A	D	C	B
12.	C	D	B	A
13.	C	B	D	A
14.	C	D	A	B
15.	B	D	A	C

Mock test 4: data interpretation

Table 5.1

1.   C

    All the other periods have at least one subsidized session during the month.

2.   B

    Addison, Baldock, Clark, Edwards, Gordon, Humphreys, Isaacs, Jordan, Lloyd, Milton, Newton and Orwell all pay full rate: 12 @ £5.00 = £60.00.

    Dickinson, Fitch and Keith all have subsidized sessions: 3 @ £2.50 = £7.50.

    Humphreys has a solo extra lesson: 1 @ £6.00 = £6.00.

    Clark and Gordon share an extra lesson: 2 @ £3.50 = £7.00.

    Therefore: £60.00 + £7.50 + £6.00 + £7.00 = £80.50.

3.   D

    Starting at 13.00: No change, remains Milton (M).

    13.30: revised to Orwell (O).

    14.00: No change, remains Lloyd (L).

    14.30: revised to Edwards (E).

    15.00 and 15.30 cancelled.

4.   C

    £212.00 / £4.00 = 53 tickets sold. 15 people = 3.5 tickets per person.

Table 5.2

5.   B

    Old fares: £180 (early July) + £230 (late July) = £410 minus new fares: £140 (early July) + £180 (late July) = £320

6.   A

    £65.00 (new tax) – £42.00 (old Tax) = £23.00 times 6731 (fares sold) = £154,813

7.   D
     Old price: £200 (July) + £250 (August)) = £450
     New price: £150 (July) + (200 – 25% = £150) (saving in
     August) = £300
     Saving: £450 – £300 = £150
8.   C
     Although the increase in fare for Tenerife is the largest
     (£100), it is not the greatest percentage increase.
     Lanzarote: new fare £275 (August) – £180 (July) =
     £95/£180 * 100 = 52.78%.
     Tenerife: new fare £300 (August) – £200 (July) =
     £100/£200 * 100 = 50.00%.

Table 5.3
9.   D
     £356.16 * 48 months = £17,095.68
10. C
     Repayment of £154.21 * 60 months = £9,252.60 +
     £598.80 difference = £9,851.40
11. B
     24 months at £454.98 will cost Mr Jones £10,919.52; all
     the others will cost him more overall.
12. F
     Without the disclosure of the variable administration fee
     this figure cannot be calculated.

Table 5.4
13. D
     The range between lowest low water (1.0 m) and highest
     high water (9.3m).
14. A
     Average low water height throughout the week for
     mornings is 1.8m; for afternoons it is 1.9m.

15. F
      Care must be taken when calculating time. The length of
      sunlight must be calculated as part of the 60 minute clock.
      Therefore, if sunset was at 18:59 (two minutes earlier than
      recorded) the daylight hours would be: 18:59 – 05:23 = 13
      hr 36 min, plus the two minutes to 1901 = 13 hr 38 min.
16. E
      A high tide 35 minutes before Liverpool would bring the
      Liverpool high tide in the afternoon into the morning at
      Southport; ie 12:16 – 35 = 1141.

Further Information

See the quickfind page on www.gov.uk for an A–Z of central government Web sites. Over 1000 sites are listed.

Other sites

www.selfassess.faststream.gov.uk
www.faststream.gov.uk
www.civil-service.gov.uk/jobs/index.htm
www.diversity-whatworks.gov.uk
www.haysworks.com

Sources of further practice material

For the Fast Stream

Books
Bryon, M (2001) *How to Pass Graduate Psychometric Tests*, 2nd edn, Kogan Page, London
Bryon, M (2002) *How to Pass Advanced Numeracy Tests*, Kogan Page, London
Civil Service Fast Stream Recruitment Report 2000-2001 (2001), Cabinet Office, London (email: faststream@cabinet-office.gov.uk)
Kaplan Educational Centres (2000) *Kaplan GMAT*, Simon & Schuster, United States

For the clerical grades

Books
Bryon, M and Modha, S (1991) *How to Pass Selection Tests*, Kogan Page, London
Tolley, H and Thomas, K (1996) *How to Pass Verbal Reasoning Tests*, Kogan Page, London
Tolley, H and Thomas, K (2000) *How to Pass Numeracy Tests*, Kogan Page, London

CD ROM
Bryon, M (ed) (2001) *Psychometric Tests Volume 1*, The Times Testing Series, Kogan Page Interactive, London

Further Reading from Kogan Page

Other titles in the *Testing* series

Career, Aptitude and Selection Tests, Jim Barrett, 1998

How to Master Personality Questionnaires, 2nd edn, Mark Parkinson, 2000

How to Master Psychometric Tests, 2nd edn, Mark Parkinson, 2000

How to Pass Advanced Aptitude Tests, Jim Barrett, 2002

How to Pass Advanced Numeracy Tests, Mike Bryon, 2002

How to Succeed at an Assessment Centre, Harry Tolley and Bob Wood, 2001

How to Pass Computer Selection Tests, Sanjay Modha, 1994

How to Pass Graduate Psychometric Tests, 2nd edn, Mike Bryon, 2001

How to Pass Numeracy Tests, 2nd edn, Harry Tolley and Ken Thomas, 2000

How to Pass Numerical Reasoning Tests, Heidi Smith, 2003

How to Pass Professional-level Psychometric Tests, Sam Al-Jajjoka, 2001

How to Pass Selection Tests, 2nd edn, Mike Bryon and Sanjay Modha, 1998

How to Pass Technical Selection Tests, Mike Bryon and Sanjay Modha, 1993

How to Pass the Police Initial Recruitment Test, Harry Tolley, Ken Thomas and Catherine Tolley, 1997

How to Pass Verbal Reasoning Tests, 2nd edition Harry Tolley and Ken Thomas, 2000

Rate Yourself!, Marthe Sansregret and Dyane Adams, 1998

Test Your Creative Thinking, Lloyd King, 2003

Test Your Emotional Intelligence, Bob Wood and Harry Tolley, 2002

Test Your IQ, Ken Russell and Philip Carter, 2000

Test Your Own Aptitude, 3rd edn, Jim Barrett and Geoff Williams, 2003

Test Yourself!, Jim Barrett, 2000

The Times Book of IQ Tests – Book Three, Ken Russell and Philip Carter, 2003

The Times Book of IQ Tests – Book Two, Ken Russell and Philip Carter, 2002

The Times Book of IQ Tests – Book One, Ken Russell and Philip Carter, 2001

Interview and career guidance

The A–Z of Careers and Jobs, 10th edn, Irene Krechowiecka, 2002

Graduate Job Hunting Guide, Mark Parkinson, 2001

Great Answers to Tough Interview Questions, 5th edn, Martin John Yate, 2001

How You Can Get That Job!, 3rd edn, Rebecca Corfield, 2002

Job-Hunting Made Easy, 3rd edn, John Bramham and David Cox, 1995

Net That Job!, 2nd edn, Irene Krechowiecka, 2000

Online Job-Hunting: Great Answers to Tough Interview Questions, Martin John Yate and Terra Dourlain, 2001

Preparing Your Own CV, 3rd edn, Rebecca Corfield, 2002

Readymade CVs, 2nd edn, Lynn Williams, 2000

Readymade Job Search Letters, 2nd edn, Lynn Williams, 2000

Successful Interview Skills, 3rd edn, Rebecca Corfield, 2002

Your Job Search Made Easy, 3rd edn, Mark Parkinson, 2002

NATIONAL
POLICE
LIBRARY